ADVENTURES IN
SCALE MODELING

ADVENTURES IN
SCALE MODELING

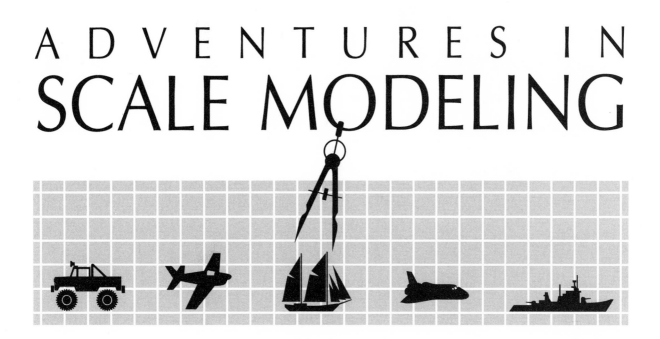

MIKE LECH AND DON GODISH

Illustrations by Ron Carboni

HEARST BOOKS

New York

It is the policy of William Morrow and Company, Inc., and its imprints and affiliates, recognizing the importance of preserving what has been written, to print the books we publish on acid-free paper, and we exert our best efforts to that end.

Library of Congress Cataloging-in-Publication Data

Lech, Mike.
    Adventures in scale modeling / Don Godish and Mike Lech.
        p.   cm.
    Includes index.
    ISBN 0-688-04575-8
    1. Motor vehicles—Models.   2. Airplanes—Models.   3. Sailing ships—Models.   I. Godish, Don.   II. Title.
    TL237.G63   1994
    688'.1—dc20   94-10690
                                                                  CIP

Printed in the United States of America

First Edition

1 2 3 4 5 6 7 8 9 10

BOOK DESIGN BY MICHAEL MENDELSOHN/MM DESIGN 2000, INC.

CONTENTS

ADVENTURES IN
SCALE MODELING

CHAPTER 1

GETTING STARTED

Read This First . . . Please

Before you do *anything,* decide on where you are going to do your model building. It may be a small space, part of a spare room, or a large workshop. Beyond some basics, there are no "blueprints" for any of these spaces. Let your own ingenuity and budget dictate how your work area will be designed. Remember, it takes more than a good workshop to build great models, and you can get by with even the most modest work area.

The three things that a model builder must have are a worktable, good lighting, and excellent ventilation. Anything else beyond these three main things is just icing on the cake. Storage areas, sinks, and other items are great amenities but aren't necessary for building quality models.

Let's further examine the table, lighting, and ventilation. The table, like an artist's canvas, is where a model builder creates a three-dimensional masterpiece. It is where models are constructed, finished, and detailed to precision. It's also the host for an assortment of tools and accessories critical to each model-building procedure.

A properly lighted work area is a necessity. Seeing materials clearly means better finished models. It's easier to concentrate on fine details when you can see them! Artists and sculptors often design their studios with windows on the south side to take full advantage of available daylight. This can also be true for your model-building area.

Ventilation is important for health and environmental reasons. Paints, glues, and other materials used in modeling require common sense and safety when using and disposing of them. A properly ventilated area protects you and the environment.

Let's look at the three main versions of the workshop: a limited space, a larger shared room, and every modeler's dream—the ultimate workshop. Keep an eye on your budget. It is always possible to improve and expand as money and time allow. Having the fanciest workshop isn't as important as developing your model-building skills and having fun in the process.

Here are some recommendations for a variety of work spaces.

THE BASIC WORK SPACE

The first requirement is a clean table area measuring at least four by six feet. Most kitchen tables will work fine. For comfort while working, the tabletop should meet your stomach when sitting. If the table is not exclusive to the hobby, always cover its surface with newspaper or an old tablecloth (preferably lint free).

LIGHTING

Most kitchens and other rooms in the house already have an overhead light. As a primary light source, they probably cast an adequate amount of light over the table. For detail work, a direct source also is necessary. A utility "clamp-on light" is a great choice to provide this light. The lamp is portable, adjustable, and puts the light where it's needed most. Most utility lights are inexpensive and use incandescent bulbs.

A fluorescent desk lamp is another choice. There may already be one around the house, but if not, they are easy to find at discount stores and yard sales. Whatever fixture you decide on, make sure it's a good source of direct, even light.

VENTILATION

Make sure the room has a window that opens to provide fresh air. The best ventilation will come from a window above the work surface. In the kitchen, use the stoves' exhaust fan to help ventilate vapors and fumes from the work area, especially when gluing or painting.

Caution: Do not use spray paint without adequate ventilation. In pleasant climates, use spray paint outside. In colder areas, install a professional ventilation system in the work area if you'll be doing a lot of spray painting.

If your work area happens to be a kitchen, remember that gas stoves have hidden pilot lights and you may need to move to a better spot for your model making.

Also, be extra careful with glues, paints, and any other material that may contaminate food products or food-preparation surfaces.

An affordable *ducted fan* can substitute for most professional systems to ventilate a work area. A ducted fan has a sealed motor that eliminates the risk of sparks. Since vapors and suspended particles from modeling supplies can be combustible if exposed to an open spark or flame, this fan is good for model building. Since this type of fan has no filtering system be sure any paints

used are safe for the environment (check labels for specific precautions).

Any temporary space such as a kitchen has drawbacks. Each time a model-building session concludes, everything must be put away. Assemblies with overnight drying time need special treatment. Devote a place in a suitable room to put these model assemblies safely away. Kitchens also sustain a lot of foot traffic, so keeping models and supplies out of the way is in everybody's best interest.

SHARED WORK SPACES

A more practical work area will be in a basement, an attic, a garage, or an extra room in the house. In most cases it's usually space that is used for other activities such as a laundry room, a guest room, or another utility area. The benefits of such rooms are that they afford better flexibility and the opportunity to leave things out overnight without moving them.

Keep space requirements in mind to design and build a table that's as wide as possible. Make sure it's no deeper than arm's length and fits flush against the wall. Again, the tabletop should meet the stomach when the modeler is seated. One-half-inch-thick Upson board is a great material for a tabletop. In fact, it's the same material used by the master model builders on the television show *Adventures in Scale Modeling*. Most lumberyards and home centers carry this inexpensive material.

If you're not up to building a table, then find one that conveniently fits in the workroom. A fine substitute, an old kitchen table, can often be found at a yard sale or used-furniture store.

A small shelf underneath the table is ideal for supplies and storage. Make sure there's plenty of room for the knees.

Note: Be sure electrical outlets are close by. There are a number of useful tools, appliances, · and lights that need electricity.

Pegboard is a good choice for the wall above the table. It's very versatile for storing tools and other useful items. Shelves are also good but can cause shadows that hamper vision while building. Both storage systems work equally well for storing parts while they dry.

Install an overhead fluorescent light fixture dead center above the table to provide even light over the work surface. Also invest in a small utility clamp light. All hobbyists appreciate good task lighting when working with small detail parts.

Note: Try to design a lighting system that produces few, if any, shadows. Shadows can be annoying and cause mistakes by hindering eyesight during tedious assembly procedures.

Be sure there is a window near the table to provide proper ventilation. Air flow is important and a ducted fan, as mentioned earlier, will help exhaust potentially harmful vapors from glues

and paints. Always remember to read and follow safety and environmental cautions provided on product packaging.

Invest in a paint booth if you can afford it! Paint booths remove paint fumes and particles efficiently and safely from the entire work area. They also filter the air and protect both you and the environment from harmful emissions. Performance, design, and cost vary, so consult a local hobby retailer or art store before buying a system. The obvious advantage of installing a paint booth is that you can paint indoors year round.

If possible, avoid working over carpet, especially deep-knap rugs. When small parts fall off the table (and they will), carpeting can make finding parts nearly impossible. Smooth, flat surfaces such as linoleum are best for floor covering in the work area.

There are real advantages to a shared work area. It provides space for some storage of tools, supplies, and extra model kits. You can leave subassemblies out overnight and let them dry without disturbing or handling them. The disadvantage has to do with *sharing* the space. People will likely enter and exit and may interrupt your work. Foot traffic can easily kick up dust that may find its way onto a model's freshly painted surface. And, if working in a laundry area, it's certainly wise to avoid spray painting near clothes.

THE ULTIMATE WORKSHOP

We have a great workshop on *Adventures in Scale Modeling.* The entire room is dedicated to the hobby and surrounds the model builder with everything the hobby needs. It is an ideal environment. Your perfect place may look different from the one on the television show, but it too will be dedicated to model building.

The dedicated room should be large. A space of twenty square feet is just about right. It will have a linoleum floor, a slop sink for cleaning, and numerous electrical outlets on several breakers or circuits.

The worktable will cover the breadth of an entire wall. Again, when the model builder is seated, the surface will be stomach high and arms-length deep. (The table on *Adventures in Scale Modeling* is designed for standing, which is best for television.) Model building takes time. We're confident that most model builders prefer sitting.

A tabletop at arm's-length depth will make it easier to reach tools on the pegboard or shelves. A wide table will let you move between subassemblies and increase the flexibility of the work.

It's important to build in easy access to electricity: Install a power strip beneath the table's front edge. This location will keep electrical cords off the table and safely out of the way.

Only your budget will limit the quality of lighting in the area. A variety of fixtures are available to choose from. Performance, function, appearance, and personal taste should guide the decision. Just remember that the goal is to produce strong illumination and few, if any, shadows.

Invest in a good paint booth. We say *invest* because this is good for you *and* the air you breathe. No matter what the weather is like outside, a booth permits spray painting without harming the environment or yourself.

A serious hobbyist will accumulate many

items, including model kits and specialized tools. Storage space will keep them organized and easy to find. Put a versatile pegboard on the wall, shelves below the table, and cabinets throughout the room. Pegboard is inexpensive and shelves or cabinets are easy to build. Old filing cabinets are also good for storage! Look around. All kinds of things are perfect for storing models, tools, and accessories.

Design the workroom to be adaptable. As you grow with the hobby, individual needs can change. You may, for example, add an air compressor and hose for an airbrush. As this and other changes occur you'll want to be able to modify the work area accordingly.

The "ultimate" work space is *only* for building scale models. It will help keep the work area neat and clean. You'll be able to move about freely from one construction phase to another. You can even include a display area or case for some of those favorite models. And, absolutely nothing will interfere or intrude upon you and your hobby.

Don't lose heart if the "ultimate" workshop is out of reach. The work space has nothing to do with craftsmanship and patience. No matter what your work area is, you can build museum-quality pieces just like the ones you see on *Adventures in Scale Modeling!*

Tools

Once you've set up your work area, it's time to equip it. How much money is spent on equipment is related to an individual's budget. The great thing about this hobby is that anyone can build fantastic models without making a major investment. Among the arsenal of supplies and tools available, only a few are essential.

By no means will every tool receive mention. What follows are those tools that can most help you to produce quality models like those seen on *Adventures in Scale Modeling.*

Note: We are intentionally omitting painting and finishing tools at this time. These tools will be examined in subsequent chapters.

A **modeling knife,** or hobby knife, is essential. Though razor sharp, it is only dangerous when misused. Children need supervision with it, as with any sharp instrument, until they display safety and skill in using the tool. There are a number of hobby knives made, but the most readily

available are X-Acto brand tools. Make sure the knife has a number-1 handle and number-11 blade. These are the most versatile and popular for building scale models; the handle is very comfortable and the blade is very useful. Ultimately, hand size and comfort will influence the final

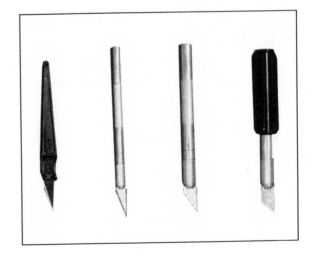

deform plastic models. Remember, unless the object is to remove a lot of material, always wet-sand.

An **emery board** is a very inexpensive and versatile substitute for sandpaper. Emery boards are great for beginners and intermediates, and experts use them, too. Take care when using emery boards; they are for dry use only and will rapidly produce heat. They are exceptionally good for corners and hard-to-reach places that require sanding.

Files. A variety of files are available. Most common for modeling are needle, rasp, and riffler files. They do the same thing as sandpaper and emery boards, and can be used wet to reach very intricate corners and cracks because of their shape. They are great for removing *flash,* which is the excess plastic left on a model kit by the molding process. It is found very often on corners and seams. Files also work well to remove material quickly, and they can create texture on a model when needed.

Razor saw. There can be a lot of cutting in model building. The hobby knife also can cut model parts by *scoring* or scribing the plastic.

choice between brands. Don't be afraid to try different sizes and styles before buying!

You are going to need **sandpaper.** It's unlikely that a local hardware store will have the kind you need. Visit a local hobby store and ask for Flex-i-grit, wet/dry sandpaper. It comes in a package that contains a variety of grits with different numerical values. Low numbers are coarse and higher numbers are fine. The paper has a plastic backing that makes it suitable for use in water. Water is important because it reduces friction, and friction creates heat which can melt and

Scoring is done by gently and repeatedly marking the plastic with the sharp tip of the knife without completely cutting through it. The piece is then snapped along the line made by the knife, resulting in a clean break.

This technique is a good one but will quickly dull a hobby knife blade. It is also easier to slip and mar the plastic where you don't want to. The razor saw is a better tool for cutting and is relatively inexpensive.

Blades are rated by number of teeth per inch. The forty-two per inch is the most popular in the hobby, followed by the 24 and 54 blades. Blades will fit a number 2, 5, or 6 hobby knife handle. This tool has many uses outside of modeling. Again, this is a sharp instrument. Respect it and handle it carefully.

Long-nose side cutters. This is a great tool for cutting off parts in hard-to-reach places. Side cutters get really close and reduce the time needed for cleaning parts. Fingernail clippers are good for beginners. Although they are not very sharp and tend to be too cumbersome for hard-to-reach areas, they are inexpensive and probably already available in the house. Eventually, you will want the side cutters.

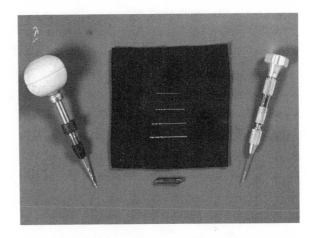

Pin-vise. This small tool is nothing more than a hand-operated drill. It comes with a variety of bits and is useful for making and enlarging holes. A hobby knife can also be used to make holes, but this method is more risky and provides less control than using the pin-vise. Drill bits for the pin-vise are numbered; the higher the value, the thinner the bit.

Tweezers. Like the nail clippers, these are probably already in the house. A larger pair is easier to use and worth the modest investment. Tweezers are great for handling small parts and decals. Fingers are sometimes too big and awkward for handling small model parts.

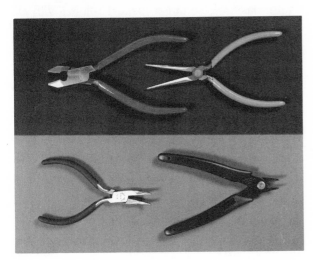

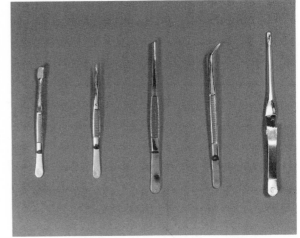

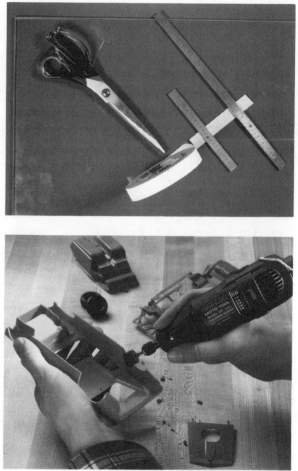

Get a box of round **toothpicks.** These have a variety of uses, such as applying glue and removing paint.

Masking tape. Besides acting as a masking material, this tape can be a great clamp. It is very effective for holding large plastic components together, and acts much like an extra hand.

Steel ruler. Provides a straight edge for the many times you'll need one. A wood ruler would be cut easily by a hobby knife.

A quarter-inch-thick, one-foot square piece of **smooth glass.** This surface is used in many situations, such as when cutting masking tape to get a clean, straight edge for detail masking. There are many more uses.

Household scissors. Cutting decals, but not too closely, is easy with scissors. They can also help make a hole larger (page 138). As with all sharp instruments, handle them carefully.

Power tools. There are a number of power tools available to the hobbyist. The most popular by far is the Dremel motor tool. The inexpensive variable- or two-speed models are excellent. This tool is best used by the advanced or expert model builder because its high speed can generate a terrific amount of heat and quickly melt plastic, permanently damaging model-kit components.

Whatever tools you acquire, keep them organized and neat. The last thing a model builder wants is to be involved in a procedure and have

to drop everything to find a needed tool. Choose a suitable storage box, jewelry chest, or carpenter's box, or use a pegboard organizer to house the tools. Try to think ahead and be prepared for the next step. A tool is only good when you can use it!

Discover other tools through trial and error, and by visiting a local hobby center for advice. Over time, you'll determine what tools you like, and which ones you dislike.

CHAPTER 2

FINDING THE PERFECT MODEL KIT

More often than not, you are going to buy model kits of subjects you like. The best selections are in military subjects, aircraft, cars, ships, and some spacecraft. Companies occasionally release specialty models, like the Statue of Liberty. These commemorative kits are available for a short time only. So, if you see one you like, don't wait too long to buy it!

It's important to consider more than just an area of interest. Keep in mind your ability and skill level. The people who manufacture model kits design them with the beginner, intermediate, and expert in mind. Many companies show skill levels on the box. We urge all model builders to select a kit that does not exceed their abilities.

The best idea for a beginner is to try a snap-together kit first. They're inexpensive and contain only a few parts. The instructions are clear, con-

cise, and easy to follow. They're also perfect for practicing assembly and finishing techniques, so that when a mistake happens it won't be on a more costly model. These benefits greatly outweigh a snap-together's small subject range and selection.

If there's a model you absolutely must have, by all means get it. There is no guarantee that those on the shelf today will be there tomorrow. Besides, many model builders bring home kits, start to build them, and realize they demand more skill than they currently possess. That's okay. Set the model aside and return to it when your skills are up to the task.

Here are some tips to make choosing a kit a little more easy.

Pay attention to *scale*. Scale is the mathematical ratio between the prototype and its model. A model car in 1/24th scale will be as large as the real thing if you multiply its dimensions by 24. Larger scales have big parts that are easier to handle. Be careful, though, because they take more storage and display space. Unfortunately, many subjects are available only in one or two scales. Companies produce model kits in popular scales for automobiles, ships, and aircraft. Cars, for example, mostly come in 1/24th and 1/16th scale.

Check, and be confident the skill required matches your ability. If the skill level is not visible on the box, then remember, smaller scales have smaller parts. The delicate methods for handling them usually create more difficulty with building the model. Keep this in mind only as a rule of thumb. Sooner or later, you'll want to try the smaller scales.

Return any model kit that is missing its instruction sheet. It takes in-depth knowledge of the prototype and years of model-building experience to complete a model successfully without instructions. Unless you're an expert, exchange an incomplete model kit for a new one with instructions.

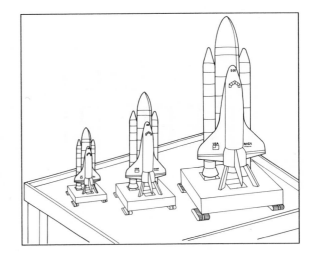

Stay with companies you know when buying your first few model kits. More established companies tend to produce kits with better-fitting parts. The result is a happier building experience—and a better-looking model when the job is done.

Model-making companies manufacture kits of popular subjects that will sell. This means that to satisfy personal interests, it becomes necessary to look for and purchase rare kits. The very nature of anything rare means it will cost more. There is also a good possibility that instructions or other items like decals will be missing or damaged. As with all models, make sure the kit doesn't require skills beyond individual ability. Rare kits are an easy find at a swap meet, in model magazines, and from specialty catalogue stores.

New model kits are available at large retailers, discount toy stores, and local hobby shops. Selection, price, and quantities will vary from place to place. Arming yourself with the useful information contained in this book ought to minimize disappointments and produce quality results.

CHAPTER 3

GET READY BEFORE BUILDING

You can do yourself a big favor by controlling your excitement after arriving home with the model kit. Immediately ripping open the box and haphazardly jumping into building the model can be a one-way trip to disaster. Careful preparation before building will reduce the chance of many errors. Enough can never be said about practicing patience with this hobby.

Always read the instructions thoroughly before building. Reviewing the instructions carefully will help you prepare for building and gathering the correct materials to complete the project. It's not possible to be too familiar with how to build a model. Remember, if the instructions are missing, take the kit back.

After reading the instructions, identify the contents. It's essential to confirm that all the parts, decals, and any other items are in the kit. The instruction sheet refers to all contents by number, and sometimes illustration.

Identify each part by using the number on the part or on the tab where it connects to the parts' *tree*. *Tree* is the term that describes the plastic area that holds the model parts together. Simply cross-reference the part number to the same number listed on the instruction sheet.

Larger parts frequently have the number molded on the part itself. Smaller parts have their numbers on a tab connecting them to the tree. It is possible that some small parts will fall from the tree and be found loose in the box.

You can identify loose parts from illustrations on the instruction sheet, or by the process of elimination. If you have many loose parts, don't panic. One way or another it is possible to identify them all.

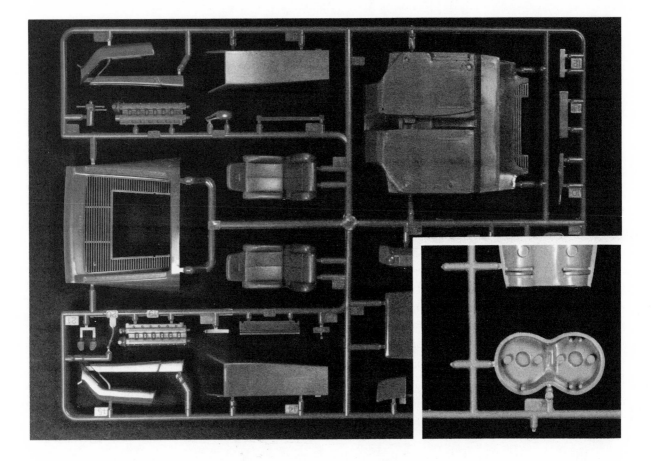

After identifying the parts, it can be helpful to separate them in bags or other suitable containers. It is too easy to misplace or lose small parts and turn the model-building project into a nightmare. Be sure to label the bags or containers with the correct part numbers. If you choose to remove all the parts from the tree, include the connecting tab to ease identification. Properly store loose parts to keep them safe and at hand during the building process.

Note: There are advantages and disadvantages to removing parts from the tree. We'll explain these in future chapters. For now, if you're just beginning, keep model parts attached to the tree.

This is also a good time to wash the model parts. That's right, wash them. When manufac-

turing model kits, the company uses a mold-release agent during the process. This material coats the metal tools that mold the model parts. The coating prevents the plastic from sticking to the tool's surface. The drawback is that some mold-release agent usually remains on model parts. With its antisticking property, the agent can have a detrimental effect on the model's finish. Washing the model effectively cleans the agent off model parts.

Take all the parts and thoroughly dip them in warm and mild soapy water. Liquid dishwashing detergent is a perfect choice for the job. Rinse thoroughly and allow the parts to air dry. Paper or cloth towels are not a good idea unless they are lint free. Lint will cling to the plastic and eventually mar the model's appearance.

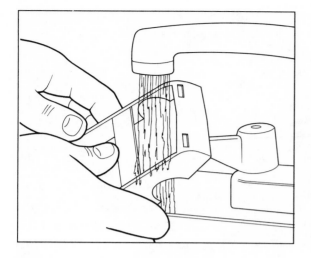

Note: It is advantageous to wash the parts while they are still on the tree. They are easier to handle and less likely to be lost forever down the sink's drain. Wash loose parts in a small pail and rinse them in a colander just as you would spaghetti!

It's not likely there will be missing parts. If the kit *is* missing some parts, it is best to return it and get another. Expert model builders often can use their skill and ingenuity to make replacement parts or borrow one from a spare parts box. If you're a beginner, it is always better to take the model kit back!

Model building can be a fantastic adventure. Go to the library, local book store, or magazine outlet and read about what you're building. You'll learn about science, advanced technologies, great historical events, and get a genuine appreciation for every model.

The scale model now becomes a vehicle for an exciting journey. When people ask about it, you can share a wealth of interesting information with them. This practical knowledge can even help you identify loose parts! A scale piston looks just like a real piston. Best of all, as Indy 500 champion Rick Mears describes, you can put yourself into the driver's seat of your very own 1/24th-scale Pennzoil PC-17 Z-7 Special Indy race car!

CHAPTER 4
TUBE GLUES

Tube glues and cements are the most readily available glues formulated for modeling. It is possible, despite a variety of other glues on the market, that tube glue is the only type many consumers may find in their area. So it is important to know how to use tube glues to construct an entire scale model.

While ideal for beginners, tube glue should not be avoided by experts. Children can immediately use the nontoxic formula and eventually move on to the faster-drying toxic variety. With either type, or for that matter any glue, always follow the precautions printed on the product label. Remember the importance of ventilation in expelling potentially harmful fumes from the work area.

Experience teaches us that controlling the flow of glue is important to successful model

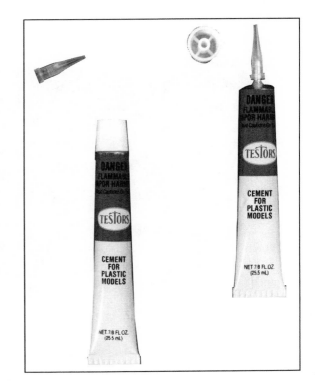

building. Tube glues and cements are thick, difficult to control, and messy when applied directly from a nozzle. The consistency, set-up time, and diameter of the nozzle can prove frustrating. Luckily, there are two effective solutions that address these shortcomings!

GLUE TIPS

The first way to use tube glue is with commercially available glue tips. The glue won't attack or *craze* these inexpensive tips made of nylon. As glue dissolves plastic and hardens, it causes deformation and discoloration. This crazing effect is most visible on clear parts as a foggy appearance, although it will show up on any exposed area of your model.

The glue tip firmly attaches to the nozzle of the tube. It is a good idea to test the tip's fit to make sure it's attached securely. The glue tip's diameter helps control the flow and amount of glue the tube dispenses. Using glue tips will decrease the risk of sloppy application and reduce the chances for crazing exposed areas of the model kit.

Hint: Though tube glues do not provide the strongest bond, it is best to always use small amounts of glue. Applying too much, even with glue tips, can cause glue to ooze from between the surfaces you are joining. Cleaning off this excess glue can be an impossible task.

USING A TOOTHPICK AND PALETTE

Because of the slow set-up time for tube glues, there is another application method that employs a toothpick and a palette. The materials needed for this technique are nearly cost-free and probably already in the house. First find a small piece of glass with no sharp edges, or a firm piece of cardboard roughly five inches square, or larger. Then get some ordinary flat toothpicks. Round ones are okay, but flat ones are easier to handle.

Use the glass or cardboard as a palette for the glue. Form a small puddle of glue on the palette about the diameter of a dime. The glue will not react with either the glass or cardboard palette surface. Then take a toothpick and simply dip the sharp end into the puddle to retrieve some glue from the palette.

Be careful not to get too much glue on the toothpick. Excessive amounts can easily drip off onto the model parts and possibly craze them.

Either glue tips or the toothpick and palette technique (illustrated on page 30) will provide the control a modeler needs when using tube glues. Practice and a little bit of patience will yield excellent results with any type of model. Beginner and expert alike will find many applications for this most commonly available glue.

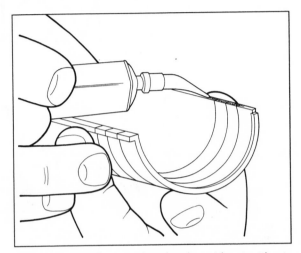

Here's an example using the tube glue with a tip. The tip gives great control and lays an accurate bead of glue along a model shuttle booster's seam.

CHAPTER 5

HOUSEHOLD GLUES FOR BUILDING MODELS

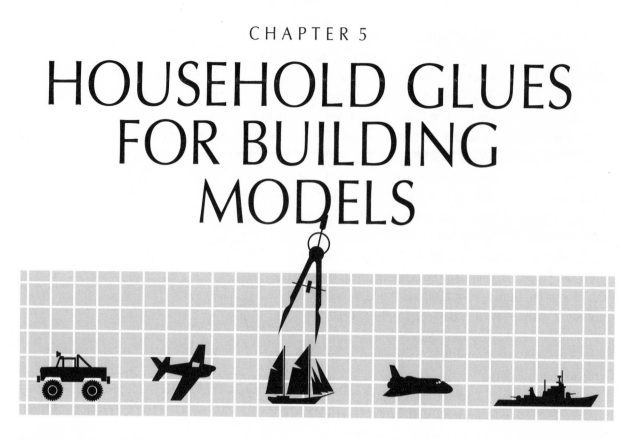

There are two household glues that are very useful in model building. These common adhesives are white glue and cyanoacrylates, the latter better known by brand names Super Glue or Krazy Glue. All of these are inexpensive and very versatile. Chances are, one or more of these glues are already in the house.

WHITE GLUE

Safe and nontoxic as a bonding material, white glue has the fewest uses. White glues set up slowly and make a weak bond. The bond characteristics make white glue unsuitable for basic construction techniques. It will prove more useful later, when we explore weathering and detailing applications (pages 61–62).

Effective in areas of low stress, white glue acts an an adhesive to bond two surfaces. This weakness is sometimes white glue's strength.

White glue does not react with plastic, and dries clear. It is ideal for any clear part like windshields, aircraft canopies, and windows.

There is absolutely no chance of crazing any clear part with white glue. If any extra glue gets on a clear part, simply remove it with water! It's even safe to remove the glue after it dries. Just remember that the bond is not strong and avoid placing pressure on parts held in place using this glue.

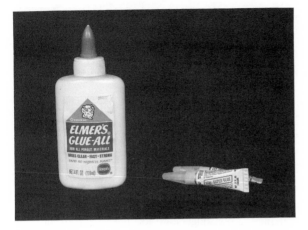

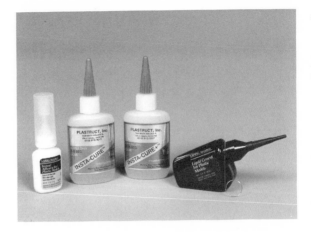

Applying white glue is easy. But the bottle is often too large, and even the ones with squeeze tips dispense too much glue. The best method for application incorporates a toothpick and palette (page 19). This provides maximum control of the amount and keeps the job neat.

CYANOACRYLATE

Cyanoacrylate is the chemical name for the adhesive in Super and Krazy brand glues. Like white glue, it acts as an adhesive between surfaces. The similarities end there. These glues are toxic and it is important to read and follow all precautions printed on the product labels. These glues can easily bond body parts to each other or to a model, so be extra careful when working with them. As always, make sure the work area has good ventilation!

Unlike white glue, cyanoacrylate sets up very quickly and provides a very strong bond. One of its foremost uses is to bond dissimilar materials. Anytime a model builder wants to bond wood, brass, or any material other than plastic, use Super or Krazy cyanoacrylate glues.

Both leading brands of glue come in very small containers and, with practice, can be applied directly from the tube to the model. If this application is too cumbersome, then use the

A good example of the white glue at work is on a model car. Here's an example of the toothpick and palette technique using white glue to install a windshield. No chance of ruining this clear part!

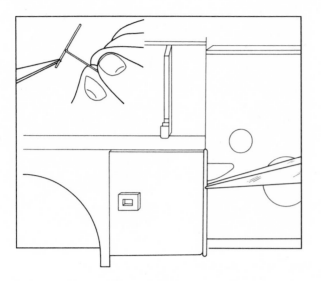

toothpick and palette technique (page 19) for these glues. Don't put too much glue on the palette. With its quick set-up time, the glue may harden before you get a chance to use it.

Here's an example using cyanoacrylate glue on a pumper firetruck model to attach a hinge made of solder. We use a small amount of the glue to bond the two dissimilar materials. When fingers are too big to act as effective tools, tweezers really help to handle the small piece of solder.

CHAPTER 6

LIQUID SOLVENTS FOR SCALE MODELS

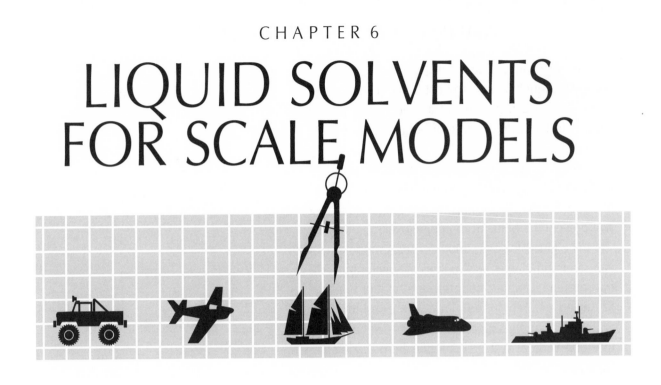

Liquid solvents soften the plastic to form a complete bond between the surfaces much more radically than tube glues. This bond requires much less set-up time and is more secure than bonds created with household glues. It's safe to say that the bond made with a liquid solvent is stronger than the plastic parts it joins!

Liquid solvents are available in hobby shops and craft stores, and from mail order catalogues. These glues are more expensive than tube glues. They are not available in nontoxic formulas. A liquid solvent has a rapid evaporation rate that accelerates its set-up time to only several minutes. This is a big advantage compared to other glues available for modeling.

As with any toxic material, this type of glue requires special handling. Remember to read and follow the precautionary warnings on the label and to maintain good ventilation. The keys to success with liquid solvents are avoiding spills, eliminating evaporation, and carefully controlling the application of the glue to the model's surface.

Liquids come in a variety of differently shaped bottles. A gentle bump can be disastrous—the glue can spill all over the worktable, tools, model-kit parts, or even on the workshop floor.

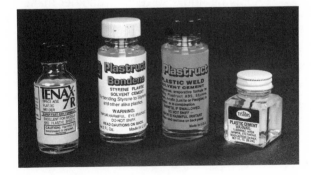

MAKING A GLUE BLOCK FOR SOLVENTS

To prevent spilling glue, take a small piece of two-by-four-inch lumber and cut it into a square block. In the center drill out a hole just large enough to facilitate the type of bottle your glue comes in.

Keeping the glue in this "glue block" provides a stable, snug platform for the bottle. In the likely event that you bump the glue, the block will prevent the bottle from tipping over.

The glue block has another use. A modeler can safely buy larger refill bottles of solvent and transfer manageable amounts to the smaller bottle seated securely in the block. The glue block will also securely support tube glues—keeping the tube vertical will prevent glue from oozing out of the nozzle or tip.

PREVENTING EVAPORATION

Loss of glue to evaporation is easy to control. Liquids evaporate so quickly that it is possible for a bottle to disappear completely in a few hours. Securely capping the bottle between each gluing session will eliminate unnecessary loss of glue.

Another good way to control evaporation is to cap the bottle loosely *during* gluing applications. Although it may seem tedious, this simple step will save both glue and money!

Applying liquid solvents is another matter. Some solvent manufacturers provide a small brush as part of the cap for an applicator. Although not ideal for everything, this brush is okay for basic applications. However, it's likely that most manufacturers will provide only the solvent.

APPLYING GLUE

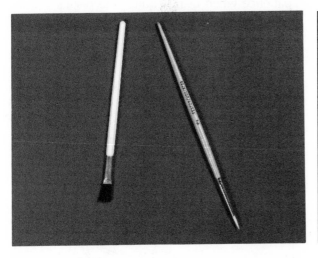

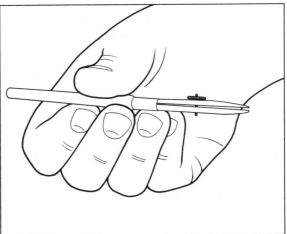

A model paintbrush is the right tool for applying liquid solvents. It is important that this brush have a metal ferrule and a wooden handle. The ferrule is the part that connects the bristles to the brush handle. Avoid plastic ferrules and handles because, as with other plastic materials, glue will attack, craze, and deform them. Why ruin an otherwise perfectly good hobby tool?

The size of the brush depends on personal preference. We recommend having several brushes with different diameters—small brushes for greater control and larger ones for applying more glue. Number-1 and Number-2 brushes are good choices.

Do not worry when the bristles stiffen from use. Caring for a glue brush is easy. Loosen the bristles by gently rolling them between your fingertips. Another method is to let the solvent loosen them naturally when the brush is dipped in the glue again.

A draftsman's ruling pen, though more costly, is another good tool for applying liquid solvents (illustrated on page 31). This instrument has an adjustable jaw that gives excellent control over both quantity and flow rate. Ruling pens, however, are not generally the choice of most modelers. When possible, experiment with different tools before making a financial investment.

Besides the advantage of a quick set-up time, liquids are also very thin. This is a great benefit because you can use them sparingly and reduce the risk of crazing your model parts. The

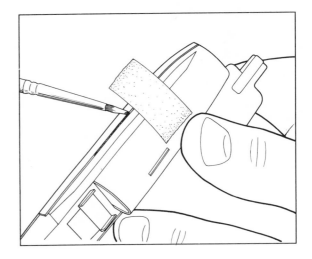

thin consistency also allows "capillary action" to carry the glue around areas for bonding. Capillary action is a property by which liquids move along a straight or curved path without deviation. Through this property, liquid solvent runs within the seam between model parts to form a clean and secure bond.

Application is simple. It's possible to use just one drop on a model plane's fuselage section, a model ship's hull, or the corners of a model building, and along a variety of other compound curves. Simply apply a small amount of liquid solvent from a brush or ruling pen and gently touch the model surfaces you want to bond. Capillary action will allow the glue to flow evenly over the entire area as if by magic.

Over time, model builders will appreciate the speed with which they can build models using liquid solvents. Remember that liberal amounts are not necessary and that set-up time for these glues is rapid. Once the bond is secure, it will be very difficult to separate the parts without damaging them. Let the size of the model parts dictate how much glue is best to use.

Liquid glues will quickly become the first choice when building. If you practice safety and patience when using liquids, the results will be rewarding!

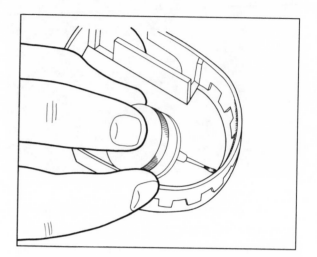

On the pilot house of this diesel tugboat it's easy to see both control and the property of capillary action at work. The solvent naturally follows the path around the model's curves, making a complete and secure bond. All that's necessary is to simply touch the brush, or ruling pen, to the surface and watch it happen!

CHAPTER 7
GLUE PENS

Glue pens are a recent development in bonding tools. Made by several different companies, the glue pen is available at some large retailers and hobby stores, and from specialty catalogues. They are inexpensive and especially good for beginners, but experts should not rule out the value of a glue pen—it can easily become an effective item in a versatile assortment of gluing tools.

Its design is simple: The glue pen is very much like a felt-tip marker, except instead of ink it contains glue. The glue is released by pressing down on its fibrous tip and then applying it to the surface. Similar to other model glues, the glue inside a pen dissolves plastic to create a secure bond between two surfaces.

A new design from a leading model company has a push button to release the glue. This dramatically improves a model builder's ability

to control the glue's flow during application. This new pen also employs a stronger, yet nontoxic, formula for the glue.

Because the glue is nontoxic and not prone to leaking or spilling, the pen is an ideal instrument for the young beginner. It works very well on straight edges and large surfaces. For pens without the glue-release button, it is necessary to go over areas repeatedly with the pen's fibrous tip to assure sufficient application.

The glue pen can be a little tedious to use on small parts. It is also sometimes difficult to control the amount of glue that disperses from the tip. Modelers will probably find that tube glues and liquid solvents will yield better control for most applications.

Because glue pens contain liquid glue, it seems reasonable to expect that glue pens will deliver the same benefits as solvents. This is not the case. Like tube glues, the glue pen is slow setting. This gives more time to work with the pieces during construction, but also slows down the building process. And unlike liquid solvents, the glue pen does not share the property of capillary action. You must physically move the pen across any area you want to glue.

Although not widely popular among expert model builders, the glue pen should be a part of any hobbyist's arsenal. Its small price tag makes it an affordable tool with which to experiment and discover novel uses for the glue it dispenses.

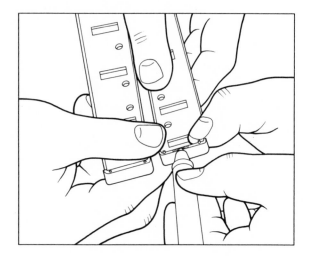

The glue pen is ideal on a flat surface or edge. Here the pen effectively dispenses glue to the lifeboats on a diesel tug model. Always scrape paint away from any model's surface to expose bare plastic at gluing points. This technique guarantees a secure bond between model parts.

CHAPTER 8

USING GLUE TO BUILD

Using tube, liquid, white, and cyanoacrylate glue is easy. Here are some practical examples from the television show *Adventures in Scale Modeling* using each type.

TUBE GLUES

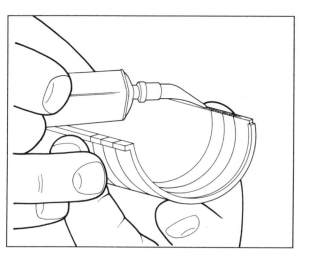

Here is an example of using a glue tip to control the flow of tube glue to a booster rocket for a model space shuttle. The long, straight area is ideal for neatly laying down a bead of cement. The glue's slow set-up allows time to adjust the two pieces to correct improper fit.

Tube glue also works on small parts. Use a glue tip to control the flow of glue. It is always best to dry-fit model kit pieces before gluing. After test fitting, use a file to remove any material causing the pieces to misalign.

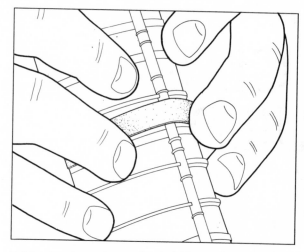

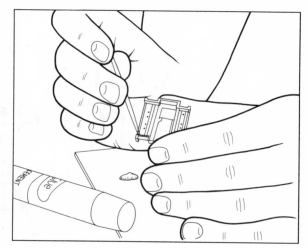

Rubber bands can be used to hold large pieces together after gluing. Be careful not to secure the bands too tightly around the parts. The object is to hold the parts firmly without creating stress that could deform the parts.

The toothpick and palette technique is ideal for small parts such as car engines. Use this method to attach manifold covers, fan blades, and other similar areas. Practice patience when doing this. Because of the slow set-up time, small area, and tiny amount of glue, it is best to let these assemblies dry overnight.

LIQUID GLUES

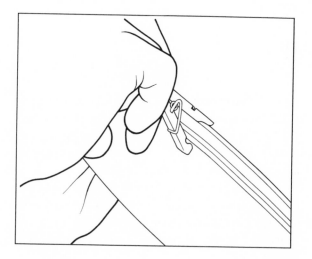

Notice the clothespins on the model? This is a great way to have a third hand when model building. Like the rubber band, this will hold the model parts in place. Correctly fit the two pieces and use a spring clothespin or masking tape to hold the parts together. On the *Star Trek* model shown here, apply liquid glue to the two halves of the ship's saucer-shaped assembly. Capillary action will carry the glue along the entire length of the seam.

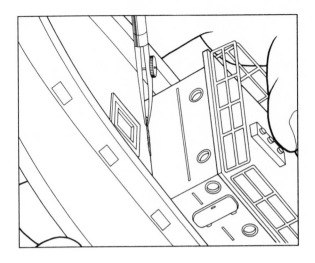

Here is an example of using a draftsman's ruling pen on a diesel tugboat pilot house. As with a brush, you simply apply glue to the part and watch capillary action move the glue. With this instrument, unlike the brush, it's possible to see just how much liquid is dispersed on the model. Once adjusted it will always deliver the same amount.

GLUING TECHNIQUES FOR CHROME DETAILS

Many models have chrome parts that pose a special problem during assembly. Model companies make chrome parts with a plating process. The chrome covers the original plastic part and therefore creates a barrier between the part and other pieces.

First it's necessary to prepare chrome model parts before gluing them. At the location of the bond, use a modeling knife, sandpaper, emery board, or file to remove the chrome material from the part.

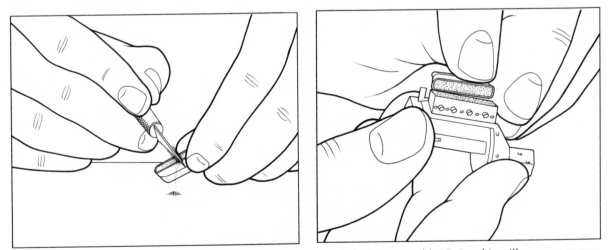

It is important to remove the chrome and reveal as much original plastic as possible. Doing this will assure a secure bond between model parts. This technique is shown here as chrome is scraped away with a modeling knife. Use a brush or ruling pen and attach the cylinderhead cover to the engine.

WHITE GLUES

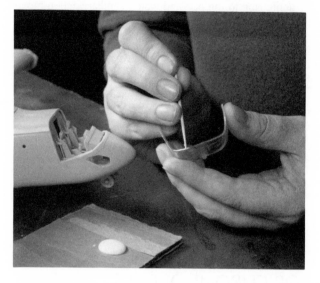

Here is an example of white glue at work. For success, first use a toothpick to apply a small bead of glue along the edge of a model windshield. Then carefully position the part in its place and allow ample time for set-up to happen. Use even less glue for aircraft canopies. Because both areas are low stress, a secure bond is not necessary. The object here is to avoid any chance of crazing clear model parts, and only to lock the pieces in place on the model.

CYANOACRYLATE

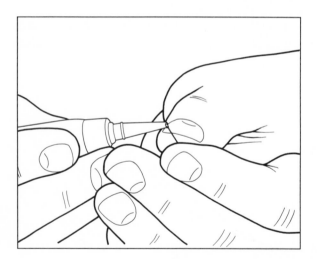

A great example of using cyanoacrylate is on the *Titanic* (pages 140–141). To attach the monofilament rigging line to the model, apply a small drop of glue directly onto the line. Use tweezers to place the rigging in its receiving hole. Within seconds, a secure bond forms. Repeat this step to attach the line to the stack. Once again, the tweezers prove perfect for holding small parts.

Anyone can have too much of a good thing. Don't use excessive amounts of glue. This only increases the set-up time and does nothing to improve the bond between the model parts. It also increases the chance for crazing external areas of the model. Over time, a model builder will accumulate a variety of glues. Practice and experimentation can lead to many uses for glues within the model-building hobby.

CHAPTER 9

FILLING
UNSIGHTLY SEAMS

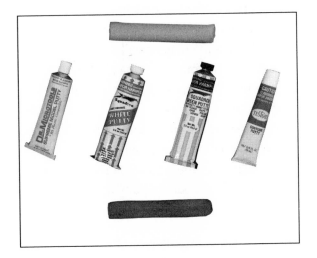

Many model companies take great pride in producing model kits that fit together with precision. Unfortunately, most model-building enthusiasts will encounter kits that are old or not made with great care. In these instances, it is necessary to make corrections for manufacturing flaws discovered while putting such models together.

The most common problem is a fit that leaves a noticeable gap between two parts. These problems frequently occur with aircraft fuselages and on similar parts with long areas to bond. Fortunately, there is an easy and effective way to correct this problem.

Much like auto Bondo body filler or dry wall spackle, a material called model putty is available to fill these gaps. This material is available at most hobby stores and from mail order catalogues. It is inexpensive and will come in handy many times.

USING MODEL PUTTY

Using model putty is easy. Squeeze a generous amount onto the seam directly from the tube. Some model builders put the putty on a palette and use an applicator resembling a doctor's tongue depressor to apply the putty. With either method, apply the putty slightly higher than the seam.

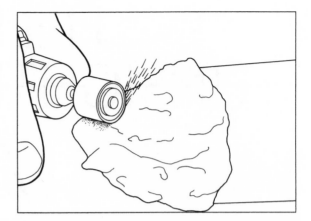

If you prefer using a motorized tool, work slowly and at low speeds. Remove the material gradually and inspect the parts frequently to assure they are not melting.

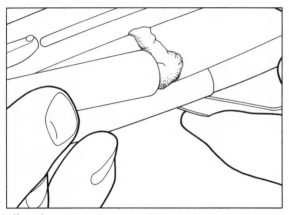

Allow the putty to dry overnight; the putty will appear dry to the touch in a short time, but most of the material below the surface is still damp. Once the putty has thoroughly dried, it is time to to finish the process.

Use wet/dry sandpaper to carefully sand away the excess putty. Wet sandpaper is better than dry, because the dry paper produces so much heat that it can rapidly remove detail from a model part and possibly deform the piece.

Wet/dry sandpapers for model building are available at some major retail stores and hobby shops, and from mail order catalogues, and can be purchased in packages that contain coarse, medium, and fine grits.

Following this procedure with care and patience will enable a model builder to successfully fill any seam. So when model parts don't fit, don't worry. Simply get out the putty and fix them!

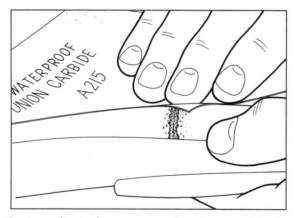

Begin sanding with coarser grits of sandpaper and slowly progress toward very fine grits. The finer grits will produce an extremely smooth surface that is ready for painting. Be generous in applying water on the sandpaper and on the model. Also be patient; it makes no sense to risk damage to the model by speeding up the process.

Experts' Choice: Experienced model builders often use a special motorized tool to remove excess putty. This requires care, and in most cases, a variable-speed tool. The motor tool operates at such high speeds that it takes only seconds to melt plastic model parts, often leaving them beyond repair.

CHAPTER 10

WHAT IS THE RIGHT PAINT?

Enamels, lacquers, and acrylics are the three most common paints used by the hobbyist. These paints have individual characteristics or properties that make them perfect for a variety of applications. It's common for the hobbyist to collect an assortment of paints, with enamels and acrylics typically getting the most use.

ENAMEL PAINTS

Traditionally enamels are the paint of choice for building scale models (although now the trend is toward acrylics). Enamel paint is basically a coating, clear or pigmented (colored), that dries through a process of oxidation and by the evaporation of its component solvents. The oxidation is a reaction between the enamel's binder polymer and oxygen in the air. Once dry, enamel paints are generally not resoluble in their original solvents. In other words, they are difficult, if not impossible, to remove.

The permanent nature of enamel paint demands careful application. The objective is to avoid costly errors that can ruin models. Working slowly and patiently will assure success when painting with enamels.

Available in a wide selection of colors, enamel paint comes in gloss, semigloss, and flat finishes. Major retailers and hobby shops will have a generous supply of enamel paints for you to choose from. Most people will be familiar with the traditional quarter-inch jars, although these paints are now available in larger, more economical containers.

Once a jar of paint is open, air infiltrates the bottle. When you finish painting, capping the jar traps air between the cap and the top of the paint. The air reacts with the paint causing oxidation and the paint "skins" over the top surface. Skinning creates a rubbery texture on the surface that slowly penetrates deeper into the paint and eventually renders it useless. Minimize this effect by storing paint bottles upside down.

There are three ways to paint a model with enamel. A model builder can brush it on, spray from a can, or use an airbrush. Which of the three methods used depends on the model type and size of the parts.

Enamel paints are slightly toxic. Read the precautions on all labels thoroughly before painting. Remember to work in a well-ventilated room, or better yet, use a paint booth. Protect your health and the environment by disposing of all paints safely and properly.

Many beginners attempt to paint an entire model with a brush. Some degree of quality can be achieved with this method, although experience teaches us that spray painting yields the best results for large surfaces such as model car bodies, aircraft fuselages, and ship hulls.

Always shake the container to mix the contents before painting with a brush or spray can. Over time, it is natural for the pigment to separate from the solvent. Shaking the container will remix these ingredients and ensure that the color of the paint is correct.

Molded ship deck details and engine blocks are examples of model parts perfect for brush painting. Some hobbyists will go through the painstaking process of masking these parts off for

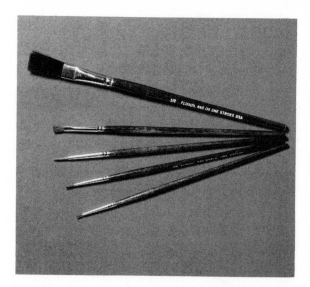

spray painting. This exhausts a lot of time and really isn't worth the effort to paint small parts in such a manner.

Go to a local hobby shop and purchase a complement of good, or if your budget permits, excellent red sable brushes. It's important to have a variety of brushes that can apply large, medium, and small amounts of paint. A "00" is a good example of a typical detailing brush. Other good brushes to have on hand are 3/0, number 2 round, 1/4-inch chisel, number 0 round, and 3/8-inch flat.

Avoid buying inexpensive brushes. They don't last as long as quality brushes and quickly develop loose bristles that can mar a model's paint job.

Model kit companies help the model builder choose the correct paints and colors by including recommendations within the instruction sheets. Generally speaking, this will provide the right colors to reproduce what is seen on the model kit's box art. It is always the model builder's option to change colors and finish the model in a manner that reflects personal taste or a different version of the model. When the instructions don't include paint recommendations, use the box art to make a match or research to identify appropriate colors.

Once you have brushes and paint, start shaking the paint bottle vigorously to agitate the paint. Then use a cotton swab stick or similar item to stir the paint, and make a rough estimate of how much paint you'll need for your first application.

Find a suitable container (a used 35-millimeter film can or its lid works well) and put the measured amount of paint from the original bottle in it. Using an enamel thinner, dilute the usable amount of paint by no more than 25 percent. Exceeding 25 percent thinner can dilute the paint excessively and affect both the color and coverage of the paint. Thinning the paint helps prevent it from covering up details molded on the model part.

Use the appropriate-size brush and remove the paint from the container or lid and apply it to the part. For large parts, move the brush in one direction only. This steady action reduces the chance of leaving brush marks on large areas. However, it will not eliminate them entirely.

After applying the paint to the part, set it aside to dry at least overnight. If you have enough time and patience, allow the parts to dry for a minimum of twenty-four hours. If the coverage appears inadequate apply another coat.

No matter how they paint, for many model builders the challenge is in handling the parts. In cases where you want to paint before assembly, it's a good idea to leave the parts attached to the tree for easy handling.

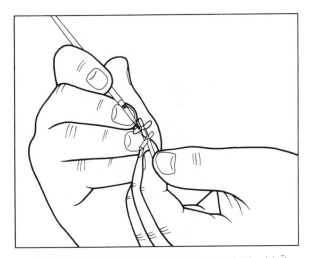

Here's an example of applying paint to a model fan blade. Note the size of brush, and that it is moved in only one direction to avoid brushstrokes. This application technique is appropriate for most small parts.

After detaching the part from its tree, clean up the area where it was connected to the tree. Then touch up that area with some paint to finish the job.

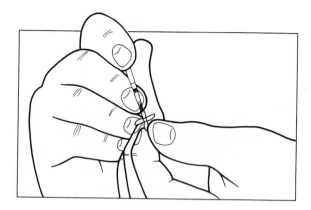

SPRAY CANS

Spray painting with cans or an airbrush provides the best finish with enamel paint. For now, we'll concentrate on spray cans and leave airbrushing for another chapter.

Spray cans, like bottles, come in a wide selection of colors. Because you are spraying fine pressurized particles into the air, there are more safety guidelines to follow. Read and observe the precautionary warnings printed on the product label. Make sure the room is well ventilated, and if possible, do your painting in the confines of a professional paint booth.

The trick to using a spray can is to avoid applying too much paint. Like paint in a jar, it is necessary to agitate the can and remix the pigment with the solvent. There should be a metal ball inside the can that moves around and helps mix the two elements together. As you shake the can you should hear the ball moving vigorously around inside. If there is no sound as you shake it, take the can back to the store where you bought it and exchange it for a new one.

The nozzles on spray cans occasionally clog. This can cause a real problem immediately after agitating the can because a clog sometimes dislodges under pressure and spews on the model while painting.

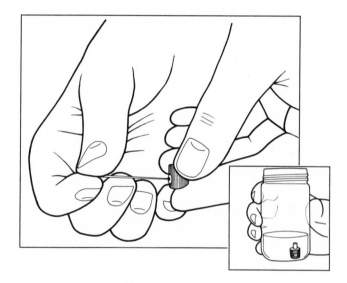

To avoid clogs, first immerse the paint can in a pot of warm (*not* hot) water. This will heat the paint inside the can and act as an external thinning agent. If you live in a warm climate, place the paint in direct sunlight and let Mother Nature warm the can and its contents.

Before beginning work, always test the paint by spraying some onto a card or piece of paper. If the nozzle is clogged, then use a small needle to probe the nozzle's opening. If this fails, take the nozzle off and soak it in some thinner. Replace the nozzle on the can and test spray again.

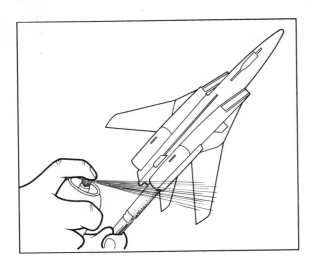

Note the use of a paintbrush handle used to hold a model part in place. It's an easy way to keep paint off hands. Using rubber surgical-type gloves is another great way to keep hands paint free. They also prohibit oils on the hand from getting on the model's surface.

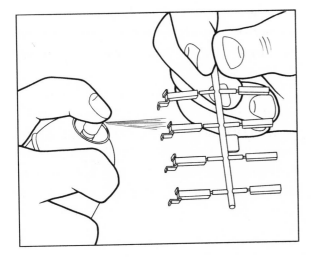

Spray painting is not only for large parts. Here are two methods for spraying small model parts. First is an example of how to leave the parts on the tree and use a uniform spray technique to achieve an even coat over everything. After removing the parts from the tree for assembly, touch up the connecting areas with a brush.

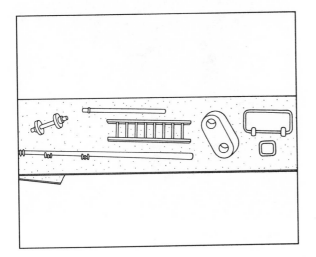

Another technique is to remove the parts from the tree, prepare them, and make a device to hold them in place. Use some masking tape folded over so it has two sticky sides, and apply it to a piece of stiff cardboard. Place the small parts securely on the tape. Then use the same spray method to paint the parts. When the paint has completely dried, turn the parts over and paint the other side, if necessary.

After you've finished painting, there is another way to minimize the risk of clogs in the future. Hold the can upside down and spray some paint onto a card or piece of paper until the can dispenses nothing more than air. Remember, warming the paint, test spraying, and removing clogs will prevent mishaps before they can ruin a model's paint job.

The correct way to apply paint to a model is to begin spraying beyond a model's surface. Once an even flow from the spray can has been established, move across the surface about eight inches above the model in a continuous sweeping motion. Repeat this process until enough paint covers the target surface.

ACRYLIC PAINTS

Acrylic paints are becoming just as popular as enamel paints. Water-based acrylic paints are enjoying greater acceptance with model builders because of the general trend toward more environmentally friendly materials.

The word *acrylic* refers to any type of paint in which the binder portion of the paint is a polymer made from esters of acrylic acids. These polymers usually contain various molecular groups that may be either thermoplastic or thermosetting systems. Acrylics can be either solvent-based or water-based.

Did you get all that? To simplify things, acrylic paint for model building will be for the purposes of our discussion a generic term for water-based paints. Mention of "acrylic" beyond this chapter will always refer to paint with this characteristic.

Most consumers refer to this type of paint as *latex*. The latex is a permanent suspension of emulsified acrylic particles. This property is why many clear acrylic paints have a milky appearance. When the paint begins to dry, the particles fuse to form a strong clear film, so don't let the appearance of paint in the bottle fool you!

Acrylics do not come in spray cans. The only ways to apply them to models are with either a paintbrush or an airbrush. Let's discuss brush

painting and follow up with airbrushing in a later chapter.

As with enamels, acrylic paint is subject to showing brushstrokes after drying. It's easy to offset this problem by thinning the paint first with water or isopropyl alcohol.

Get a large container to collect some rain water to thin the acrylic paint. Rain water is soft—meaning it contains few minerals—and this helps reduce the "surface tension" of the paint. Surface tension is what causes paint to bubble up on an area by impeding its flow across a model's surface.

The effects of surface tension.

It's also easy to soften tap water by adding some liquid dishwashing detergent to it. Mix one drop of detergent per one ounce of water and thin the paint with this solution.

Mix acrylic paint the same way you would enamels. It shouldn't be necessary to dilute the paint any more than 25 percent. Experiment until you discover a ratio that produces the best results.

After thinning the paint, use the appropriate brush and apply paint to model parts using the same application techniques used for enamels. Again, it is important to paint in one direction. In this example, a small-tip sable brush effectively applies paint to create the distinctive Y on the USS *Yorktown*. Notice the even finer-tip brush applying a custom paint scheme on the Chaffee tank.

CARING FOR BRUSHES

A model builder's paintbrushes are valuable hobby tools. Preserve and protect brushes by cleaning them properly. Using the appropriate thinner, solvent, water, or alcohol, gently swirl brush tips within the solution. Take care not to push the bristles into the bottom or the side of the container! Slowly pull the brush out of the container and drag the bristles gently along the container's lip. Then take some white tissue paper and fold it around the ferrel and bristles. Roll the ferrel and bristles inside the tissue paper between your fingers. Make sure that no paint remains be-

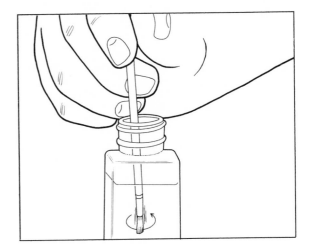

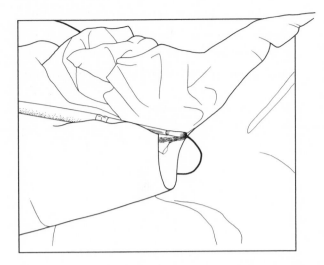

tween the bristles by repeating the above steps until the tissue shows no color from any residual paint. If the brush comes with a protective plastic tip, use it to protect the bristles until you're ready to paint again.

LACQUER PAINT

Lacquer paint is another choice for scale models. Lacquer is a coating, clear or pigmented, that after application dries solely by the evaporation of its component solvents. Unlike enamels, it is always resoluble in its original solvent. This means that once lacquers dry, you can remove them with a liquid solvent similar to the one that was originally in the paint.

Model builders generally use lacquer paints to apply base coats on large surfaces. Instead of being found in hobby shops, an assortment of lacquers is most often available in hardware stores and auto parts shops.

Lacquers come in both regular cans and spray cans. You also have the option of thinning lacquer paint for use in an airbrush. The techniques for application are the same as for enamels.

There is a word of caution to follow when using lacquer paints with scale models. The chemical composition of lacquer sometimes attacks plastic. This is commonly referred to as "etching." The paint literally melds into the plastic and can mar a surface.

If you are going to use lacquers, test the paint first on the underside of the model. If the etching effect is pronounced, consider using enamels or acrylics for your project.

No matter which paint you choose, work on days that are not humid or rainy. Moisture in the air will prevent the paint from drying evenly and will dramatically increase the drying time. This often creates an unsightly appearance for the finish on your model.

Among enamels, acrylics, and lacquers, a model builder will discover a wide range of paint colors. Many companies that make paints use the federal standard number as a cross-reference. With this number it's easy to accurately select from a broad range of colors to get an exact match. All major model paint companies use federal standard numbers. Most, if not all, instructions include paint information. Research will also often reveal the federal standard numbers for the specified paint scheme. With practice and patience you'll be able to achieve superb results!

CHAPTER 11

CHOOSING, CARING FOR, AND USING THE AIRBRUSH

Among all of the tools available to model builders, few rival the airbrush for producing great-looking finishes. For one reason or another, model builders are reluctant to invest in and use an airbrush. But after using one a few times, it quickly becomes evident why this tool often heads the list of every serious hobbyist's equipment arsenal.

An airbrush disperses paint in the same fashion as spray cans do. This is where the similarities end. Spray cans have the advantages of requiring no cleanup, needing little preparation before use, and being inexpensive. The limitations with cans are the choices of spray patterns, which have to be confined to a wide area or be circular, fewer color choices, and ultimately their higher cost over the long haul. Remember, only three ounces of paint costs about three dollars and the wide spray pattern a modeler is forced to use creates a lot of overspray!

An airbrush does exactly what a can does. It sprays paint. The advantages are a nearly endless choice of colors (it's even possible to mix colors), a variable selection of patterns, and excellent control of paint flow. The great control means less time for masking and the ability to lay down fine coats of paint that produce a superior finish.

An airbrush system doesn't have to be an expensive proposition. Years ago, this was true because the only airbrush models available were made for professional artists. Today, many companies produce versions with the hobbyist in mind. These systems range in price from twenty dollars for the most basic up to two hundred dollars for professional models. An investment of

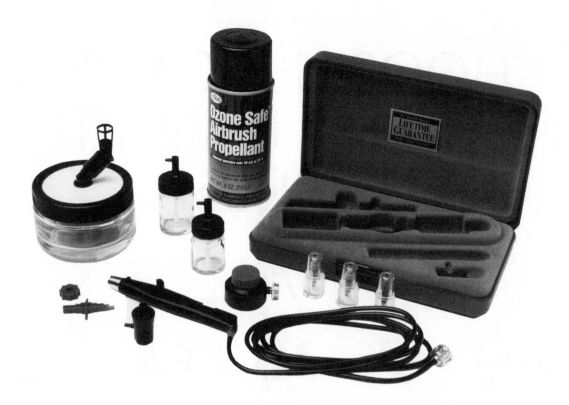

about eighty dollars will get you a good airbrush capable of years of service. It doesn't take a lot of spray paint cans to add up to that figure!

What should a person know about an airbrush before buying one? Designs vary so be sure to handle the instrument to see if it feels comfortable in your hand. It's also necessary to choose between a single-action unit or a double-action airbrush.

SINGLE-ACTION AIRBRUSHES

The single-action airbrush mixes paint externally. An operator controls the flow of air through the airbrush with a trigger, and the system works by moving the air above a siphon tube coming from a paint bottle. The air mixes with the paint externally, passing through a needle to land on the model.

With a single-action airbrush the operator must *stop* painting to adjust the spray pattern. Ex-

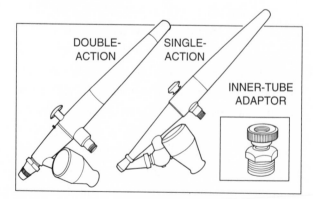

cept for the least expensive models, rotating the the tip of the brush will widen or narrow the spray pattern. With many models there will be a generous selection of needles in different diameters to choose from. Select a variety that provides a good range of spray patterns.

DOUBLE-ACTION AIRBRUSHES

The double-action airbrush combines the single-action process into one step. The trigger moves up, down, forward, and backward. The up-and-down motion controls the flow of air. The forward-and-backward motion controls both pattern and paint flow. With this system the paint and air mix internally so the operator can control the double-action process.

The double-action airbrush is more expensive but saves precious time by adjusting pattern and flow during the painting process. Like the single-action airbrush, it has an assortment of needles that provide different spray patterns. Recent designs use interchangeable nozzles instead of needles. Changing the nozzle is quicker and easier than changing a needle.

GENERATING PRESSURE

The other important item for consideration is the choice for source of pressure. Often, newer airbrush systems will come with a can of propellant. Can propellants are easy to find and most are ozone safe. However, they are probably the most expensive way to deliver air to an airbrush system.

The air in cans is extremely cold. It is very possible for an airbrush to freeze up at the air's exit point. Avoid this problem by immersing the can in warm—*not* hot—water while painting.

Another source of air is a spare tire or inner tube. Many hobby shops will have spare tire adaptors that work with an airbrush. Obviously, this is a very cheap source of air. The drawbacks are the inability to regulate the air and the drop in pressure while painting.

CARBON DIOXIDE (CO$_2$)

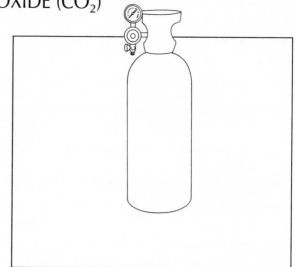

Carbon dioxide, or CO$_2$, is another source of pressure. CO$_2$ is inexpensive and easy to get. It's vital to practice care when handling this pressure source because it is volatile. As with supplying pressure with a spare tire, it is necessary to purchase a CO$_2$ regulator for your particular airbrush from a local retailer. The CO$_2$ provides a good, regulated, consistent source of pressure to the airbrush. When the tank empties, take it to a qualified dealer for a refill.

COMPRESSORS

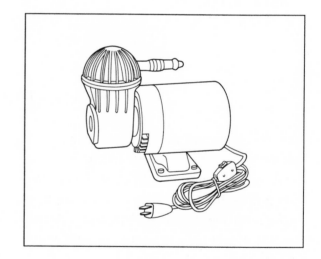

Undeniably the best source of air comes from a compressor. These machines come in two designs: piston and diaphragm. Piston compressors, which need occasional lubrication, are less expensive than the diaphragm types. The advantages of diaphragm compressors are they have fewer moving parts and will need less ongoing maintenance.

For an average of about one hundred fifty dollars, either system is a good choice. Unlike other sources, both will provide a limitless amount of pressure. If you plan to airbrush often, invest in a tank designed to stabilize and control pressure. Once the tank is filled with air the compressor works much less and suffers less wear and tear. External tanks that attach to compressors are available at automotive stores.

Virtually any kind of paint is suitable for use in an airbrush. Except for the new "ready to use" types, all paints need thinning before use in an airbrush system. How much paint should be thinned is really a personal choice. It will depend on the color, the coverage the model needs, and what mixture works best for a particular airbrush. Experimentation is the best word of advice here.

Because airbrushes use any kind of paint, the choice of colors becomes nearly infinite. If a color is not available, it is possible to mix others to create the desired shade. Only "ready to use" paints, which cost more, limit the selection.

MAINTAINING AIRBRUSHES

Like any fine tool, it is essential to clean and maintain an airbrush after every use. Vigilant care will assure the airbrush remains an effective part of your arsenal of tools.

First connect the appropriate thinner to the airbrush and run it through the system. This process will remove any residual paint.

Disassemble the needle, following the instructions for your particular airbrush. Bathe all the component parts of this assembly in more thinner. Put the needle in a separate container to assure a thorough cleaning. Reassemble the brush components and run thinner through the system once again.

Test spray onto a light cardboard surface and look for any residual paint. If using white paint or other light colors, use a darker piece of cardboard for this test. Then store the airbrush in the case or packing material it came in.

Here are a few more suggestions for using and maintaining an airbrush system.

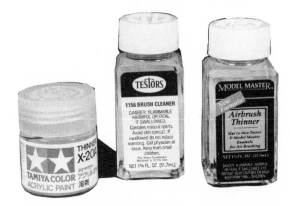

- When the airbrush is brand new, first test it with the thinning solution you plan to use (water or solvent, depending on the paint) to make sure it is clean and working properly. It's a good idea to repeat this step each time before starting to paint. This will prime the airbrush, and the operator can be confident it's ready to use.
- At the end of every painting session clean the airbrush thoroughly. With some models this can be as easy as using a cleaning station. If your airbrush doesn't have one, then follow the cleaning instructions that accompany it. When changing paint colors, run some thinner through the airbrush until it produces a clear spray pattern.

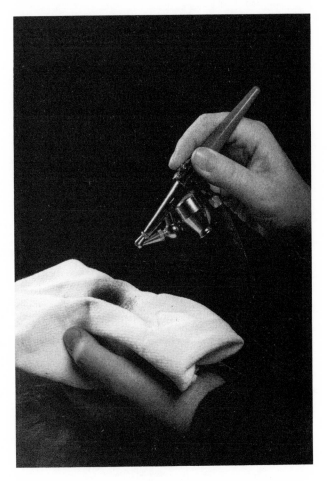

• Periodically inspect the needle for any deformities that can cause a malfunction. These may appear as cracks, dents, or similar physical damage that can affect the spray pattern.

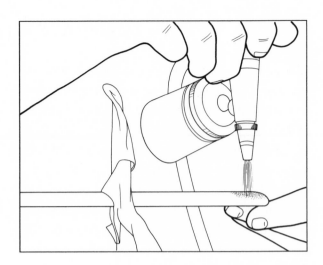

Here's a good example of using the airbrush. The model builder is painting the tip of a wing using little masking while controlling the flow and pattern with the airbrush. The light coats reduce the risk of any paint seeping beneath the masking tape.

CHAPTER 12
DECAL APPLICATIONS

Painting is generally just one step in the process for adding a professional finish to your scale models. Most aircraft, ships, cars, spacecraft, and other models include decal sheets for interior and exterior details. Decals are colorful, distinctive, and the perfect finishing touch for many scale replicas.

Decals also present the opportunity to duplicate the exterior details of an existing or historic prototype. For example, let's say you are building a Boeing 737 airliner and the kit's decals include United and Delta airlines. But suppose, for authenticity's sake, neither United nor Delta operate airliners that fly within the region you intend your model to be situated in.

To find decals that aren't included in the original kit, a model builder needs to contact a specialty catalogue company. These companies

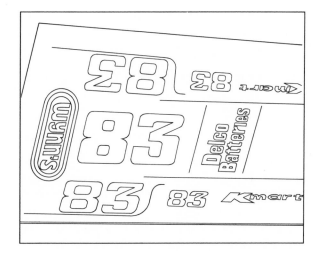

advertise in specialized publications devoted to modeling. A typical catalogue's selection of decals will include many airline names, different race team names, military armor markings, and a variety of commercial and military aircraft decals.

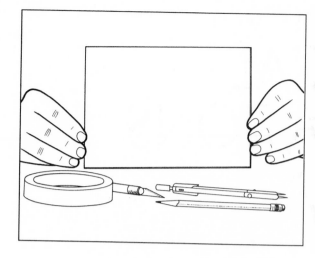

If a particular catalogue store does not stock the decals you want, there is another alternative. Undecorated color and clear decal sheets are available at many hobby shops. With these plain decal sheets it is possible to duplicate any name or logo design for a model. Though not as easy as ready-to-apply decals, creating homemade versions can often be worth the effort (pages 104–105).

Many model builders are nervous about applying decals because they seem delicate. There really is nothing to fear when applying decals. Some careful preparation and a few simple ap-plication tips should lead to consistent success.

A decal will look best when applied to clean and glossy surfaces. This doesn't mean that decals should never be applied on a flat or matte finish. If the model has a matte or flat finish there are ways to improve the decal's final appearance.

A glossy finish prevents air pockets and *silvering* from occurring underneath the decal. Silvering happens when a decal doesn't lie flat on a surface. This creates visible, silver-white air pockets between the decal and the model that ruin the appearance. This effect becomes even more pronounced on flat finishes.

PREPARING AND POSITIONING DECALS

Prepare the decal by trimming off the excess paper around it. You can safely use a small pair of sharp scissors or a hobby knife to cut out decals. Some model builders keep their scissors sharp by reserving them just for decals. Work carefully with either tool to reduce the chance of ruining the decal by accidentally cutting it.

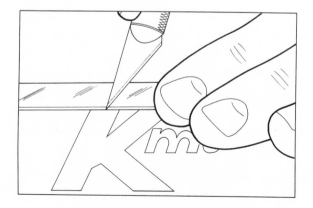

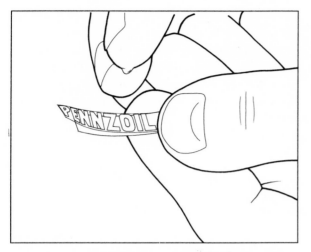

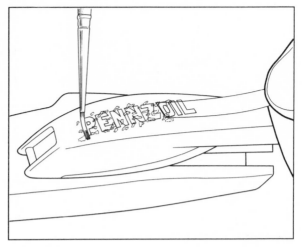

Next, soak the decal in clear water until it floats on top. Another way to test and see if a decal is ready for mounting is to gently move the decal a little and see if it slides freely away from its backing paper. When this happens, take a brush and gently scrub the decal to remove any excess adhesive. The adhesive keeps a decal only on the sheet, not on the model.

Spread a generous amount of water on the model in the area where the decal goes. Using tweezers or a small brush, remove the decal completely from the backing paper and place it on the model.

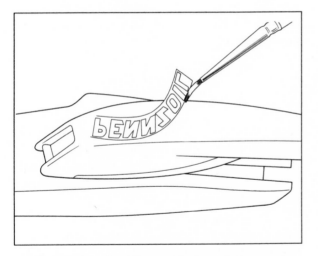

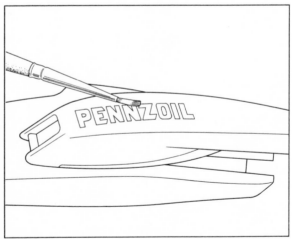

Don't worry if the decal flips upside down during transfer. Gently use the brush and work slowly from end to end to turn the decal on the correct side. Some people like to use their fingers instead of a brush for this step. You'll probably discover that your fingers are too big and awkward to transfer and position decals effectively. Tweezers and a small brush will work better to transfer and position decals.

Using a brush (or fingertips if you really prefer), carefully move the decal into proper alignment. This has to be done by eye and knowledge of where the decal goes. The model's box art, instructions, or photographs will help pinpoint the exact position.

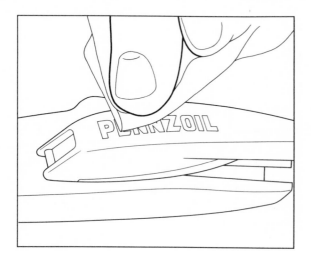

Remove the excess water with a paper towel. Softly pat the decal with the paper towel until it absorbs most of the water. Inspect the decal to make sure it is still in the correct location. Before a decal completely dries, you can adjust the position by wetting it and repeating the above steps. Once completely dry, it is no longer possible to move the decal.

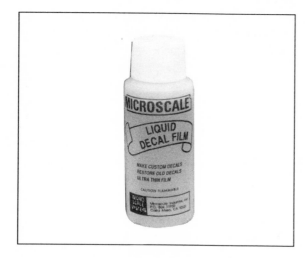

After patting it dry and confirming the correct position, apply a thin coat of decal-setting solution. This product softens a decal and allows it to snuggle down on surface details or imperfections, and helps eliminate any layering appearance the decal may cause. This same solution also improves the final appearance of decals on models with a flat or matte finish. Be careful when using this material. Decal-setting solution is a solvent that turns decals into a gel-like material. Any attempt to move decals after applying the solution will probably result in irreparable damage.

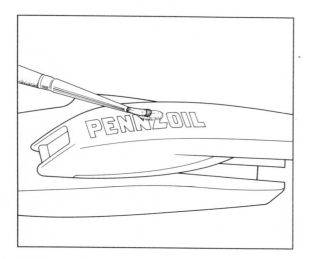

Let the decal dry for a minimum of twenty-four hours. Apply the remaining decals following the same procedure. When the last decal dries, one final step remains. It's a very good idea to apply a clear coating, gloss or flat, over the model's entire exterior.

Spraying or brushing a light clear coat will seal the model's entire finish and provide protection for the decals. It also will help to eliminate the trim lines of the decal film. Now you are ready to proudly display your scale masterpiece.

CHAPTER 13

CAMOUFLAGE AND WEATHERING TECHNIQUES

Camouflage and weathering a model depend heavily on research. Facts about a model's prototype will help a model builder apply these techniques more effectively. Camouflage is an application more common to military subjects, while weathering techniques can apply to any type of model. It is another example of the personal flexibility model builders enjoy when creating their scale replicas.

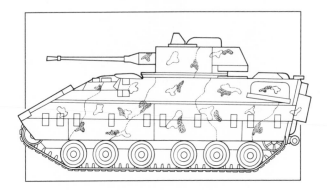

CAMOUFLAGE

Camouflage is an effective way to conceal or blend an object within its environment. In real life, the military uses camouflage to protect its soldiers and equipment and to surprise its enemies. Applying camouflage schemes to models can be done using three basic painting techniques. Depending on personal preference and skill level, camouflage can be applied with a brush, a spray can, or an airbrush. The weakest delivery system among these three is the brush.

If the intent is to duplicate a paint scheme that has a feathered edge, then an airbrush is a necessity. Both the spray can or paintbrush will create hard edges between colors, which may or may not be an accurate representation. Refer to page 113 for complete details on applying camouflage paint schemes.

WEATHERING

Weathering is the effect that age or natural elements have on the exterior appearance of a model's prototype. This can appear as faded paint, rust, dirt, or other physical scars. A popular technique for creating some of these effects employs the application of "wash" solutions. A wash solution is a very dilute mixture of paint or another material and thinner. Depending on the composition, this solution can cause an appearance that artificially fades or ages certain exterior parts of a model.

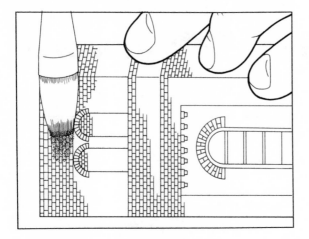

Later chapters will discuss in detail a variety of techniques for weathering using washes, artist chalks, sandpaper, and other materials. For now, the most important thing to remember is not to apply any weathering technique with a heavy hand. Light applications will ensure a realistic look no matter what material is chosen for creating the effect.

The effectiveness of camouflage and weathering relies on the skills of each model builder and the quality of visual reference materials. Before attempting any of these techniques, it is wise to test them. Using a piece of plastic from an old model kit or some similar material to practice not only tries out the technique but also improves the chance for success when applying the material to an actual model.

CHAPTER 14

RESEARCHING MODEL SUBJECTS

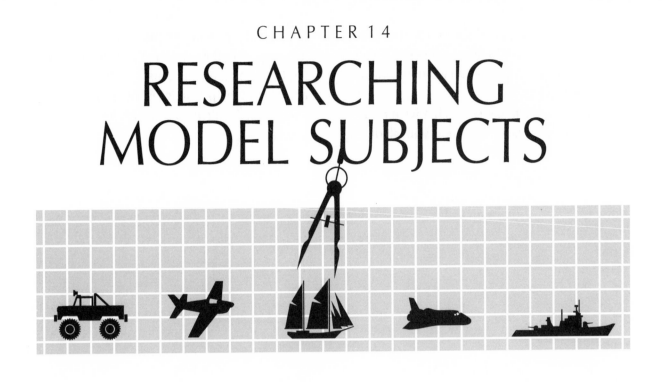

When first starting out in this hobby, it is quite rewarding to build model kits just as they appear on the box. Eventually, as individual model-building skills improve, an area of interest will often develop, and the object then becomes one of creating exact replicas of real prototypes. To accomplish this takes good, authoritative information about the prototype.

Model companies try to help by providing background information inside their kits. The facts are useful, but space severely limits what they can provide in the kit. Reading and research are the best ways to learn about what you are building.

Research will produce photographic information that helps emulate paint and camouflage schemes. Other details can reveal how to weather the model, where to make modifications,

which colors accurately duplicate the prototype's appearance, and where distinctive markings, such as decals, go.

Research may also raise the model-builder's level of knowledge and the context of a prototype in history. Such information is also useful during model competitions and for displays.

There are several excellent sources of information about a model's prototype. *Mary Jane's Defense Weekly* and *Squadron Signal* publications are perfect for military buffs. There are numerous publications for the automobile and aviation enthusiast. And countless books contain thorough information, with valuable color or black-and-white photographs.

Visit a local library, bookstore, or hobby shop to find research material about a special subject. Don't ignore opportunities to see the real thing at a museum, air show, or car show, or in a harbor. Remember to take your camera! A picture really is worth a thousand words when building scale models.

It's possible to get research advice by writing to the manufacturer. Many will gladly respond with press information materials that can get a model builder well on the way. When writing to these companies, address the letter to the attention of the public information office. Be adventurous: Don't limit yourself to just one resource.

CHAPTER 15

DETAILING MODEL CARS

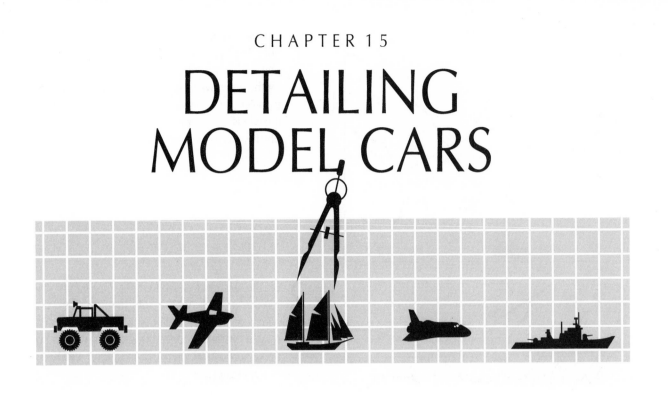

Model builders often build a model kit as it appears on the box. This is fine for many hobbyists, especially beginners, but as skills and abilities progress, most hobbyists depart from this approach. There are many ways to add greater detail and distinction to cars and other type model kits.

A model builder can do this using any number of techniques. Careful use of paint, Bare-Metal foil, sandpaper, and even auto wax can create exquisite details. Let's share some easy ways to get fantastic exterior and interior details.

WINDSHIELDS

A showroom car always has a shiny windshield. The problem with plastic is that it does not effectively replicate the high gloss of glass. Floor wax can add a glasslike appearance to a model kit's plastic windshields and other clear parts.

Besides creating the look of glass, the wax will help remove small scratches. It also acts as a protective barrier to prevent scratches from appearing when you handle the parts. This technique is appropriate for clear parts in any model kit except in those instances where the objective is not to produce a high-gloss finish.

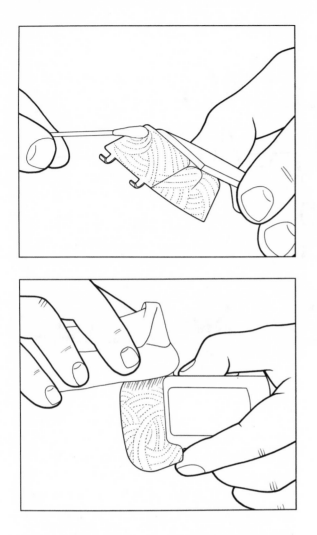

1 Purchase, or find around the house, a liquid household floor wax. The brands Future and Minwax are perfect for this job. Use a plastic lid as a palette for the liquid wax. Apply a small amount of the wax to the end of a cotton swab. Gently apply the wax to the windshield using the cotton swab. Be sure to apply the wax to the interior and exterior surfaces.

2 Let the wax dry to a white, hazy appearance. Then remove it gently with a soft, lint-free cloth. Even with a coat of wax it's possible for lint to create a scratch on clear model parts. Continue buffing until the windshield attains a high-gloss finish that resembles real glass.

Just as on real glass, scratches will ruin the appearance of clear model parts. Minimize minor surface scratches by using a mild polishing compound for difficult scratches that the wax can't remove. But remember that an overly abrasive compound will only add to the problem. If a windshield or other clear part appears irreparable before polishing, return the kit to the dealer for a replacement.

SEATS

A great-looking windshield is an invitation to look inside a model's interior. The most eye-catching interior details are the seats. Here's how to make great-looking new seats or old worn ones.

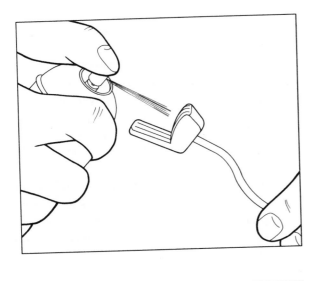

1 A two-tone seat can be a challenge to duplicate. First, spray or brush paint the seat in its primary color.

Model parts are often easier to manipulate with an effective handle. Make a handle by gluing an appropriate length of sprue to the underside of the seat. (*Sprue* refers to any tubular section of the parts tree made as plastic flows to create the model parts during the mold-making process.) Don't worry about scarring the bottom of the seat. After installation, the underside is no longer visible to the eye.

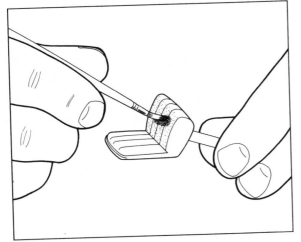

2 Once the base coat dries completely (typically, three or more hours), apply the accent color. Using a small detail brush, apply undiluted paint to the seat. Reduce the number of brushstrokes by always painting in the same direction, but remember, it's nearly impossible to eliminate brushstrokes completely.

Repeat these steps for the other seats, and when the paint has dried completely, install them according to the model kit's instructions.

If you choose to spray paint the accent color, it is necessary to mask off the seat, and for such a small area, this can be a very tedious task. Use thin pieces of tape so they will conform to the compound curves of the seat.

LEATHER ENHANCEMENTS

Classic and luxurious automobiles usually have rich leather appointments such as seats and dashboard coverings. Fortunately, many companies help simulate this appearance by molding texture details into the model parts. A model builder can easily enhance this built-in detail with a few simple steps.

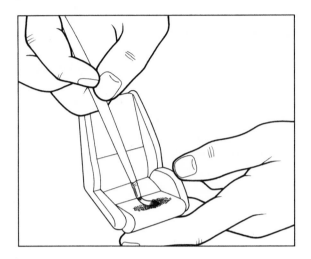

Acrylic water-based paints seem to work best as washes. The acrylic will not react with an enamel or lacquer-based paint and comes off easily with water before it dries. The wash will not harm an acrylic base coat as long as the base coat is completely dry.

Another method for getting the appearance

Using the holding stick, paint the seat a shade lighter than the color you want the finish to be.

Next, mix up a solution to make a *wash* that is darker than the color initially applied to the seat. A wash solution is a paint mixture that is mostly thinner. A 35-millimeter film container is the perfect place to mix a wash. The best method to test the solution is to experiment with the underside of the seat until reaching the desired effect.

Brush the wash on the seat generously, making sure to get it into any molded cracks or crevices. Remove any excess wash by drawing it off the model part with a brush. When the wash dries, it will produce the effect of leather folds and shadows on the seat.

of great-looking leather seats is to apply a coat of flat black, or another color. When the first coat is completely dry, spray on a very light coat of clear semigloss. At first, the appearance will be very shiny, but once dried, the surface's shine will tone down and the seat will have the soft glean of new leather.

MAKING MODEL HOLDERS

Here is another effective way to hold a seat, or other model parts, while painting. On a large piece, such as the one shown here of a Ford Model-T bench seat, simply tape a long cotton swab stick to the bottom. On smaller pieces, attach the stick using a cyanoacrylate glue, such as Super Glue or Krazy Glue, to secure the wood to the plastic. Remember, cyanoacrylate glue is the right choice for bonding dissimilar materials.

   To make a companion drying station, take a block of wood and drill out holes to receive the diameter of the stick. After painting a model part, place the stick into a receiving hole to hold the piece safely until it dries completely.

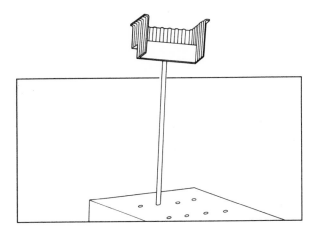

   Not everyone wants a model car's interior or exterior to have a new-car look. Most real automobiles will show some visual sign of wear and tear. Here's an effective way to simulate worn leather seats.

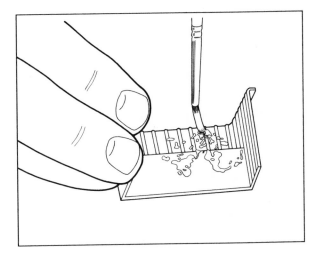

1 Get some white glue, water, dishwashing detergent, and facial tissue.

   Prepare a 50/50 percent mixture of white glue and water. Add a couple of drops of dishwashing detergent to reduce the surface tension of the water.

   Use a quarter-inch or similar-size paintbrush and generously apply the white glue mixture to the seat.

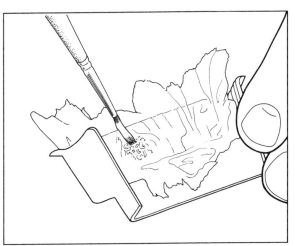

2 Tear the facial tissue into pieces to place on the seat. Do not substitute toilet paper for this step because it breaks down in water and will not be effective for this application. Use the brush to position the tissue in the corners and over the edges of the seat.

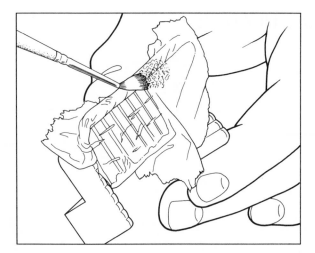

3 Apply more of the glue and water mixture on top of the facial tissue. This will assure a secure bond between the tissue and the seat. Place the seat into a drying station and let it dry overnight.

4 When completely dry, spray paint the seat a color of choice. When the paint dries, the seat will have the appearance of aged leather with customary cracks and wrinkles.

SIMULATING RUBBER TIRES

Most model car kits come with shiny rubber or vinyl tires. Besides this unnatural shine, they also have a seam line that runs down the middle of each tire. Detailing and weathering tires can add dramatic and realistic details to a model car's exterior appearance.

Here's how to weather the tires and give them a "run over the road" look.

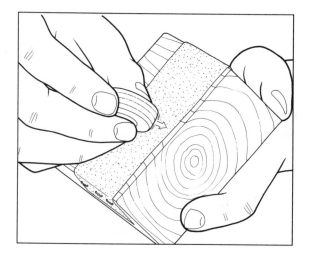

Make a sanding block with a small piece of two-by-four and medium-grit sandpaper. Wrap the sandpaper around the block of wood and secure it with staples or thumbtacks. The block provides a uniform surface for many sanding operations.

Rub the tire tread across the sanding block to remove the seam line. An emery board can substitute for the sanding block. With either tool, be sure to sand in the direction of travel, not perpendicular to the tread pattern. You can also try lightly sanding the sidewalls to create scuffs for a worn and dirty look on the sides. The tires may even be made to have the appearance of scraping a curb or two.

LETTERING TIRES

It is not uncommon for a model kit to have tires with embossed company names, like Goodyear or Michelin. The challenge is in effectively duplicating raised white letters without marking the rest of the tire. There are several ways to tackle this.

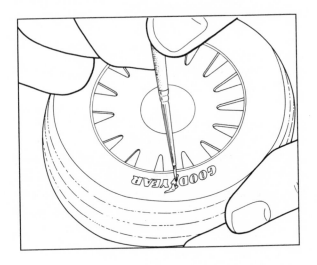

1 Get some white water-base acrylic paint and a fine detail brush, such as a number 3/0. Carefully paint the letters with the acrylic paint. Don't worry if the paint gets outside the embossed areas. The components of acrylic paints and the rubber tires make cleanup easy.

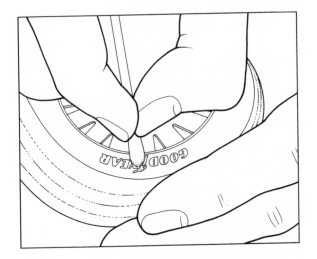

2 Take a damp cotton swab and gently rub it across the top of the embossed letters or logo. Be careful not to press too hard. Use the raised areas to prevent the cotton tip from removing paint inside the letters.

Continue removing all excess paint from the tire's sidewall. If necessary, touch up any area inside the embossed letters with the white paint and the number 3/0 brush.

When cleanup is complete, the tires will have a perfect white raised-letter appearance. This technique is only effective on those tires that have an embossed or raised edge around the letters.

Sometimes a model's tires will come without any company markings. When this happens, it is still possible to create the white raised-letter look on a set of model tires (see pages 64–65).

DRY-TRANSFER LETTERING

An "after-market" product known as Shabba Tire Decals is available at many hobby stores and from mail order catalogues. This product is nothing more than dry-transfer letters that come in a variety of tire company names and logos. They are an effective and easy way to get white company lettering on a tire. It also is a good substitute for any model builder uncomfortable with the previous painting technique.

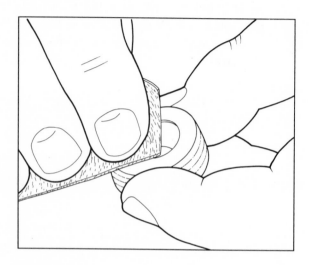

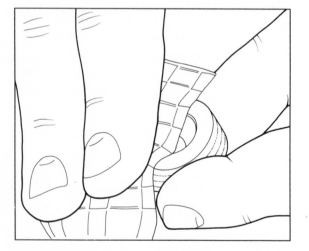

1 Dry-transfer letters work best on a smooth, clean surface. A tire without an embossed name requires little preparation to have the correct surface texture. Just wipe off the tire with a cloth to remove excess dirt or other foreign material.

The model builder must remove embossed letters by rubbing the sidewall of each tire with sandpaper (left). This process will cause a dull finish on the tire's sidewall. Use a soft cloth and buff the tires to restore their original luster (bottom left).

2 Prepare the dry-transfer letters by warming them for a few moments under a low-watt light bulb or hair dryer. This gentle heat loosens the adhesive and makes the transfer easier to apply on the tires.

Cut only the name from the sheet for transferring to the tire. Position it on the tire using reference photographs or the box art to find the correct location.

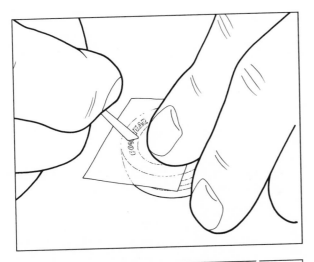

3 Rub or burnish the letters on to the tire using a brush handle or burnishing tool (left). Slowly pull the backing paper away and check for any part of a letter still on the sheet (bottom left). Continue burnishing until each letter transfers completely over to the tire's sidewall.

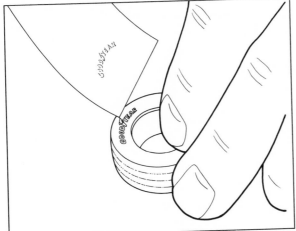

Automobiles and trucks, more than any other model types, come with ready-to-use chrome parts. Following the earlier technique for assembly (page 31) will assure success with chrome-plated plastic. There are instances, though, when a car or truck kit will have parts that need a chrome finish. When this happens, it is time to use a product known as Bare-Metal foil (see pages 66–67).

CREATING THE APPEARANCE OF CHROME

Bare-Metal foil is a micro-thin foil that comes in silver and gold. It has an adhesive backing that makes it easy to apply on model parts.

Because it is so thin, the foil is a bit hard to work with but it doesn't obscure any molded-in details. Here's how to use the Bare-Metal foil.

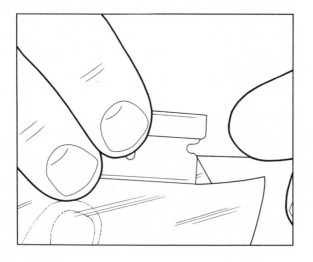

1 Measure the area on the model that the foil will cover. With a fresh blade in the hobby knife or a razor blade, cut the foil slightly larger than the area it will cover. Use very little pressure, letting the blade do the work. Avoid cutting through the backing paper of the foil.

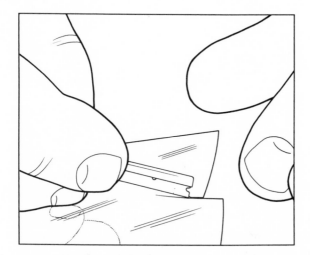

2 Once the foil is cut, use the tip of the blade and carefully lift one of the edges. Set the blade safely aside.

Take a pair of tweezers and slowly pull the foil away from the backing paper. Be careful: Moving too fast can tear the foil! Use your fingers if the tweezers don't work well.

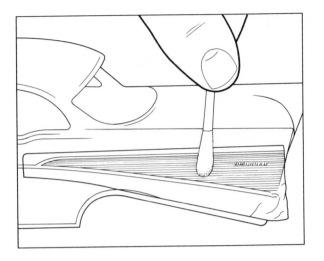

3 Apply the foil to the model part. Use a dry cotton swab to burnish the foil over any details and contours of the model. Don't use a damp swab. Water reacts with the foil and creates an uneven, dull finish.

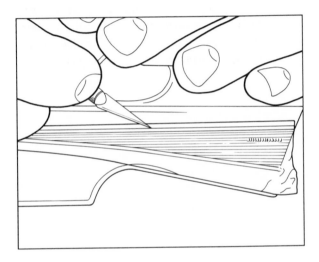

4 After burnishing the foil over any details and contours, use a hobby knife and carefully cut off excess foil. Let the contours or other molded details guide the blade to avoid damaging the model's surface.

Carefully use the tip of the blade to lift a corner of the excess foil and use tweezers to remove remaining foil.

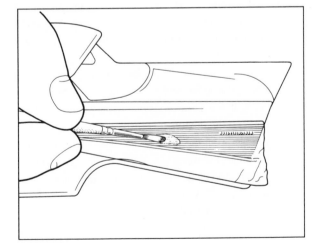

5 Burnish the edges with a dry cotton swab to complete the job. Applying a thin coat of clear acrylic paint will create a dull aluminum finish.

This technique is great for adding chrome details around windshields and headlight wells, on door handles, or on any other part needing a chrome finish. Be willing to experiment with the foil. The results will be worth it!

ENHANCING ENGINE DETAILS

Many model-car builders like to show off the machinery under an automobile's hood for everyone to see. The engines of model cars, trucks, and other vehicles have many interesting details, and with a few basic techniques, it is simple to produce an engine that is deserving of its very own display space.

Avoid assembling an engine before painting it. Car and truck engines have seam lines that the paint will cover up and painting engine parts before assembly helps maintain authentic-looking seams between manifolds, on the engine block, and in other engine areas.

Here are some more ways to bring out great engine detail.

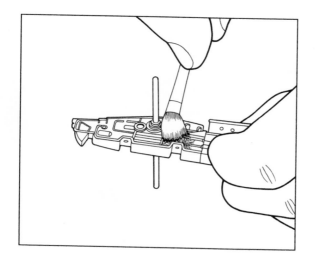

1 Select the appropriate color and then paint the parts using a "scrubbing" technique. Place a liberal amount of paint on the brush and use the scrubbing action to get the paint into all the molded details. Then set the parts aside to dry completely.

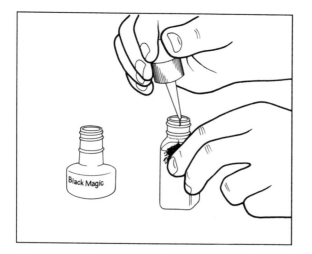

2 Use an india ink wash solution to accent corners and shadow areas. Acrylic or enamel washes are fine, but it's often easier to clean up excess amounts of india ink. India ink is compatible with any type of paint.

Get a clear, clean glass container, like an old paint or glue jar, and add isopropyl (rubbing) alcohol to it. Put a few drops of india ink into the jar and stir. Test the mixture by brushing a small amount on a fingertip. If the wash reveals good fingerprint detail, then the mixture is correct. If the fingerprint's detail is too light or obscure, then adjust the mixture accordingly: Add more ink to increase detail and more alcohol to decrease detail.

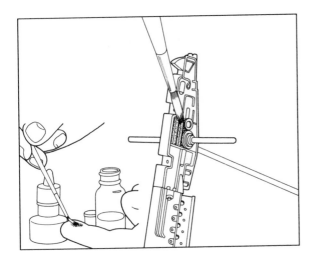

3 Take a brush and scrub the wash solution on the engine. Be sure to get the solution into every nook and cranny on the engine. The object here is to accentuate those deep shadow areas. Set the engine assembly aside to dry completely.

If the result is unsatisfactory, or too heavy, use some isopropyl alcohol to remove the excess wash solution. It is possible to remove all the wash and start again until the desired effect is achieved.

Once the engine dries thoroughly, it is ready for more detail work. Adding shadows is not quite enough to create a superb-looking engine. Highlights will bring out any molded details such as automaker's name, bolts, and other fine features.

DRYBRUSHING

There are three materials that work really well to create highlights. They are SNJ powder, antiquing pastes, and artist's pencils. The powder and antiquing paste are applied to the model with a dry- brushing technique. Drybrushing refers to a technique that allows you to remove nearly all the powder, paste, or paint from a brush before application. Here's how it works.

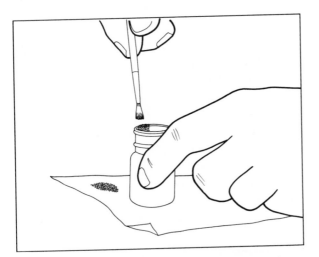

1 Remove some powder from its container with a paintbrush. Run the brush across a paper towel to remove as much powder as possible.

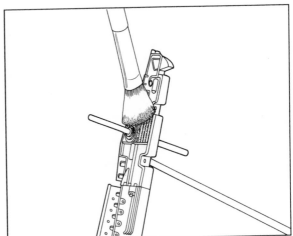

2 Select the area to highlight and lightly whisk the brush over the top of the detail. Note how the details pop out and add depth to the engine.

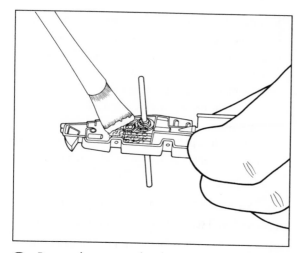

Drybrushing is very susceptible to smudging and finger marks. Once the process is completed, be careful handling the model parts.

If you choose to "drybrush" with paint, dip the brush into the paint and then flick as much of the paint as possible from the brush onto a piece of cardboard, a rag, or tissue paper. Then, lightly whisk the brush over the part to be detailed.

3 Repeat these steps for the antiquing paste. Paste tends to stay on the brush and will probably seem heavier and less easy to apply than the powder, so be sure to remove as much as possible using the paper towel. Keep applying the paste until the highlights are satisfactory.

PENCILING ON HIGHLIGHTS

Another way to bring out highlights is with an artist's pencil. This process is simple and a great substitute for anyone not comfortable with drybrushing.

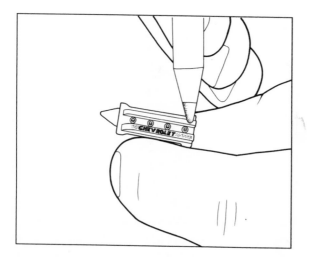

Identify the area for highlighting. Shown here, it is the name *Chevrolet* on a model engine block.

Choose the appropriate color pencil. In this case, the correct color is silver.

Gently rub the side of the pencil tip along the top of the word *Chevrolet,* rubbing lightly to reduce the chance of creating highlights that are too heavy in appearance. Remember, it's always easier to add more material than to remove it later.

As with the powder and paste, the pencil also can smear. Take extra care when handling parts and also during final assembly. The application of a clear coat will afford some protection, but the best advice is to avoid excessive handling.

DETAILING LIGHTS

Model-car headlights and taillights are dominant exterior features. The challenge facing a model builder is to replicate the appearance of a real lens. The common approach is to paint the outside of the plastic lens the appropriate color— red, yellow, etc. This is okay for color accuracy but does nothing to simulate a real lens.

A better idea is to paint the back of the piece. The thickness of the model part will yield some modest effect of depth. Still, it falls short of the ultimate goal of simulating a real lens.

The best approach is to use a combination of translucent and silver paints to replicate headlights and taillights. To achieve a realistic look, follow these steps:

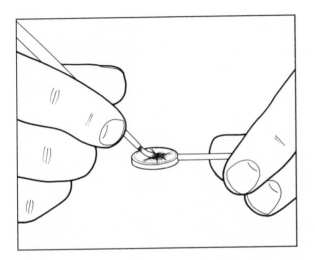

1 Get some red translucent paint. For ease of handling, paint the underside of the part while it is still attached to the tree. Painting the underside takes advantage of the clear part's natural depth and enhances its glasslike appearance.

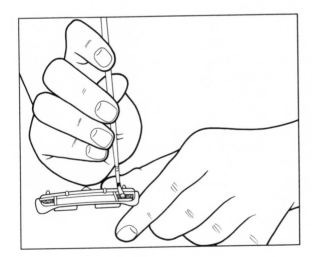

2 Use silver paint for the car body's taillight well. The paint creates a reflective background resembling the shine on a real car. (A piece of Bare-Metal foil can substitute for the paint.)

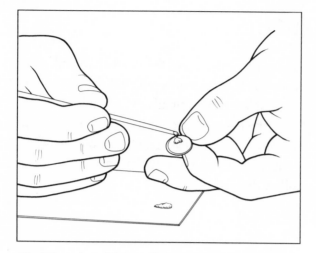

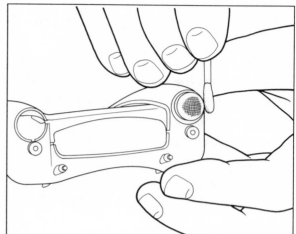

3 When the taillight well dries, install the lens using white glue. Remember that white glue dries clear and won't detract from the effect you're trying to achieve. Some model builders who are unhappy with the performance of white glue like to use clear epoxy instead. Although it also dries clear, epoxy glue is more expensive and requires mixing before use.

4 For headlights it is only necessary to paint the headlight well silver. Then install the lens in the same manner as the taillight. Use a cotton swab to remove excess glue.

DETAILING CONVERTIBLES

When building model convertibles it is challenging to simulate vinyl, canvas, and cloth tops. Model companies try to help by texturing the roof's hard plastic surface. This often looks good but there are a few other techniques that make a model look more authentic. Here's how to replicate a vinyl roof.

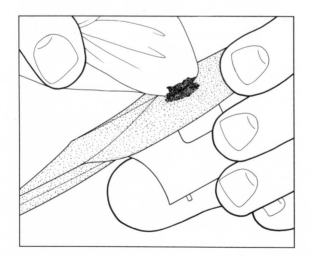

Paint the roof the color you want. A historic Ford Model-T roof is black. Get some shoe polish that matches the roof's color. Shoe polish is a wax and will buff to a rich luster that simulates vinyl.

Apply the polish to the roof with a soft cloth and rub in small circular motions.

Let the polish dry and then buff it with a clean, soft cloth. If the roof has any molded texture, the shoe polish treatment will enhance its details and make the top look like real vinyl.

Here's how to simulate a canvas or cloth convertible top:

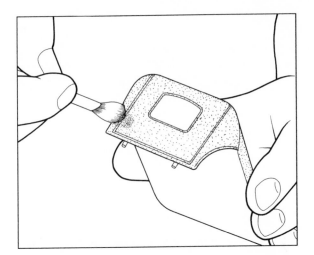

Paint the roof using the appropriate color. Take a large brush and apply some translucent facial powder (available in jars from a drug store that stocks cosmetics) on the roof. Remove any excess by shaking the roof over a piece of paper. Apply more powder if too much falls off.

The powder gives the roof a soft, clothlike look. The powder coating, however, is not permanent. This means that any handling can ruin the effect achieved with the powder. If this happens, simply reapply the powder, repeating the entire process.

"FACTORY" PAINT JOBS

No model car is complete without an excellent "factory" paint job. To accomplish this effect you can use brushes and paints, spray cans, or an airbrush. Brush painting is the least desirable choice for painting such a large area because no matter how careful you are, brushstrokes will inevitably appear on the final finish.

The best methods for painting model-car bodies and other large model parts are to use spray cans and airbrushes. Each system delivers smooth, even coats of paint. They also come in metallic finishes that are perfect for cars and trucks.

METALLIC FINISHES

Few exterior finishes rival the look of metallic paint. Yet, to get great results there is more involved than just spraying paint over a model. Here are some important guidelines for working successfully with metallic paints.

Before applying metallic paint, it is important to note that there are metal particles in the paint that will settle on the bottom of the container. To prevent this, you must frequently agitate the can or the airbrush siphon jar before and during painting.

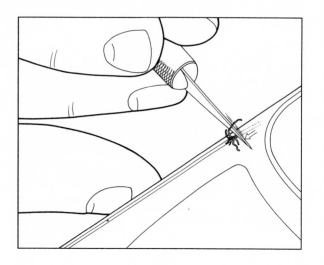

1 Metallic paints will reveal all flaws and lines on a model. To eliminate this problem it is necessary to prepare the model's shell properly before painting.

To remove all seam lines left from the molding process use a hobby knife to scrape along the seams to even them out. *Adzing* is the term that most often describes this technique.

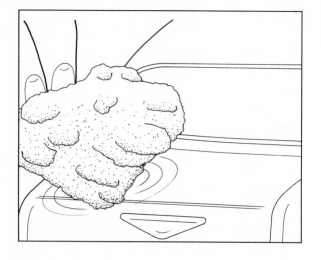

2 Next polish the model with fine steel wool. Polish in a circular motion to prevent the wool from scratching the surface. The steel wool will polish out any minute scratches or gouges that metallic paint would otherwise accentuate.

Wash the model and your hands to prevent any risk of dirt or body oils remaining on the model that may later harm the paint job. Let the model air dry in a dust-free area. It is not a bad idea to handle the model with gloves or a lint-free cloth after it is clean.

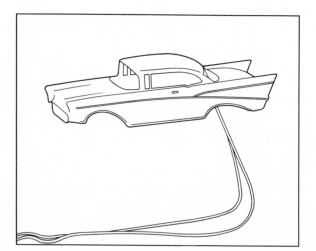

3 Since the model's body shell is quite a large piece, it may be difficult to handle. To make handling it easier, fashion a holder using a metal coat hanger. Untwist the hanger's hook and bend the hanger into a straight piece of wire.

Now bend the hanger back at the center, and then bend it again so it roughly conforms to the contour of the model's shell. The tension of the metal should hold the model part securely in place.

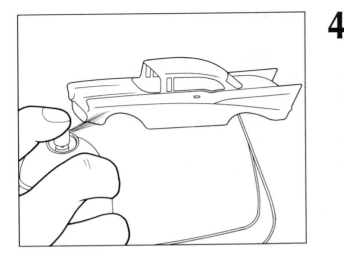

4 Apply a base coat of silver or gold enamel to the body's shell. Metallic paints are translucent and need a base coat; the silver or gold will help enhance the paint's metallic look.

Test spray the metallic paint and begin to apply light misting coats to the body's shell. Move in smooth, even strokes over the model. Wait at least twenty minutes between each coat. Continue applying the paint in light mists until the desired coverage is achieved. After reaching 100 percent coverage, set the model aside to dry overnight. Use the coat-hanger holder to suspend the model in a safe location.

Building the paint up in misting layers takes full advantage of the translucent properties of metallic paints. Spraying in heavy coats can cause runs or drips, and destroy the translucent metallic effect. On close inspection, a metallic paint job should have a really deep finish color. Only patience and very light coats applied over time will guarantee results that resemble the finish on cars as they appear on a showroom floor.

LARGE-SCALE MODELS AND TRUCKS

Large-scale model cars and trucks don't need painting. Yes, you don't have to *paint* every model to get a good-looking car or truck. Larger scales, especially those larger than the traditional 1/24th scale, have so much body surface that painting even becomes a less desirable choice in some instances.

When a large-scale model comes in a suitable color, it is simple to transform its raw plastic surfaces into ones with great-looking finishes. To do this use progressive grits of wet/dry sandpaper, and any one of the following: plastic polish, automobile polish, rubbing compound, or toothpaste.

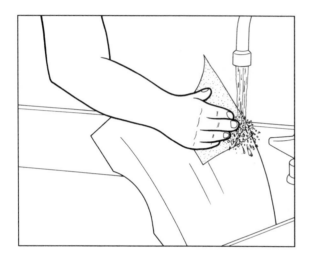

1 Wet-sand the model, working progressively to finer grits of sandpaper. Each grit will remove successive scratches and other exterior flaws. Working with wet paper, or even under an open tap, will reduce the heat that friction generates. Remember, if plastic surfaces get too hot, it's possible to deform a model! Eventually, the finest grit will produce a smooth finish with a dull appearance.

    Rinse the model thoroughly to remove any foreign particles left by the sanding process.

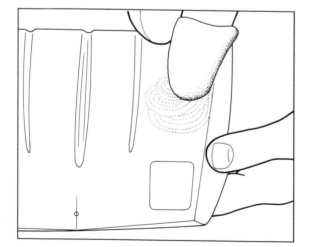

2 Using a polish of choice, take a soft, clean cloth and apply it to the model. Use a circular motion and continue rubbing in the same way until any scratches left by the sanding process are removed.

    Let the body shell dry to a haze.

    Get a soft, lint-free cloth and buff the model's shell. Continue buffing until you are satisfied with the model's shine and exterior finish.

CREATING RUST ON MODELS

Pickup trucks, construction equipment, and off-road vehicles seldom look brand-new. These rugged work vehicles typically have a rusty or dirty appearance in real life that a model builder can easily replicate. This "weathering" technique is great for fenders, grillwork, wheel wells, or anywhere else dirt or rust may collect.

Airbrushing, drybrushing, or artist's chalks are the best devices for making rust. Chalks are by far the easiest to use, but it never hurts to experiment with other techniques. Here's how to use artist's chalks to create a weathered look.

When creating the effect of rust, keep nature's forces in mind. Rust will move under the influence of wind, rain, and gravity. So make sure the rust is falling downward and in the direction that other forces, such as motion, will influence.

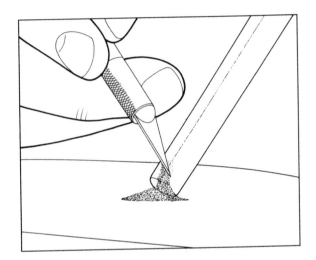

1 Gather together a selection of chalks that resemble the color of rust. Take a hobby knife and make a powder by scraping a small amount of chalk on to a paper towel.

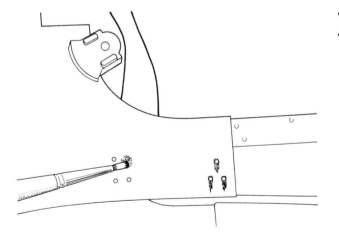

2 Find an old brush that is no longer suitable for painting. Any size will do, but don't use a good brush for this job.

Dab the brush into the pile of chalk powder you created, and sparingly apply it to the area where you want the rust to appear. (Here, it is applied to the bolts of a D8H Caterpillar model.) Blow off any excess powder from the model.

Remember, the chalk's powder is not permanent and handling it can ruin the effect. Apply a flat, clear coat of paint with a spray can or airbrush after weathering the entire model. The clear coat will ensure that the powder and other weathering applications stay in place.

USING PAINT TO CREATE RUST

If you don't want to use chalk to create the effect of rust on a model, use spray paint to accomplish a similar effect. This is particularly good for large areas such as the tracks shown here on a Caterpillar earth mover.

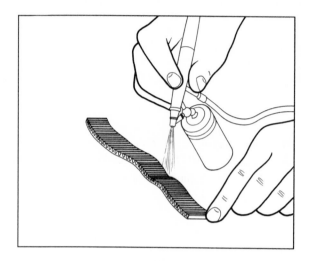

1 Select a paint color that resembles rust. Spray paint the area you want to treat in uneven coats. The uneven coats will more closely simulate rust as it would naturally occur.

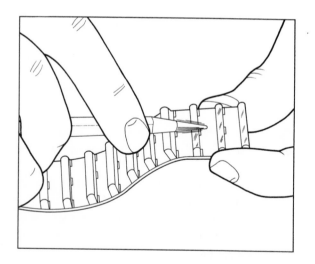

2 An extra detail that adds distinction to a model is one that replicates bare metal. As shown here, the metal will be bare wherever the tracks strike rocks or other hard objects. To create this effect, use an artist's silver pencil and rub it along any high edges. In the example here, this creates the bare metal appearance the tracks would have on the real machine.

DIRT AND MUD

Dirt and mud are other weathering techniques that look great on construction and off-road vehicles. As with rust, simulating either of these materials on a model is not hard. Here's how:

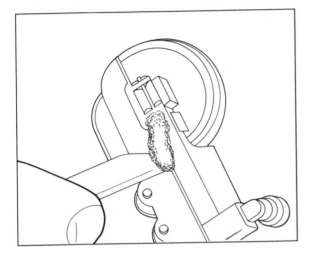

Decide what kind of dirt or mud you want on your model. It may be topsoil, clay, or sandy soils. Choose a paint that closely matches the color of the dirt or mud. Typically, use reds for clays, shades of brown for topsoils, and tans for sandy soils.

Blend a 50/50 mixture of paint and baking soda. Stir until the paint and baking soda are completely mixed.

Use a small, flat applicator, like a Popsicle stick, and apply the dirt or mud to the model. The blade on a bulldozer model, fender wells, and bumpers are typical locations for mud.

After applying all the dirt or mud, apply a clear coat of paint to secure the materials to the model.

RACE-CAR DECALS

Race cars, more than any other type of model, rely heavily on decals for exterior details. Most kits will come with a complete set of colorful decals to match a favorite race-team's name. There will be times when duplication of a particular team will require after-market decals.

After-market decals provide the opportunity to change a Kyle Petty Mello Yello Pontiac into a Rusty Wallace Miller Pontiac. These different team names come from mail order sources as either registered or unregistered decals.

A registered decal has all the colors, including borders and shadows, on one decal sheet. An unregistered decal has the primary names and logos on one decal sheet and the borders and shadows on a separate one.

Here's how to change a 1989 Wynn's NASCAR Oldsmobile into the same year Kodak racing version using unregistered decals:

1 Prepare a clean and glossy surface on the model in the place where you want to apply the decal.

Soak the first decal sheet in water. (Here we're using the red number four.)

Liberally wet the surface of the model at the location of the decal. (Here, it is the roof of the car.)

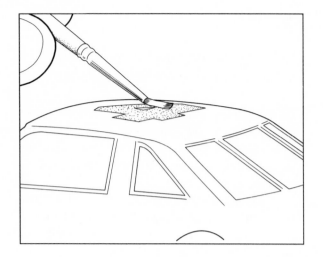

2 Place the red numeral four down on the roof following the basic techniques for decal application (pages 50–52). Do not apply decal-setting solution at this time.

Placing the color numeral down first makes it easier to align the registration lines that create a black border.

Let the first decal dry overnight. It is important for the first decal to be completely dry before applying the next one. A damp decal will move on the surface and make it impossible to correctly align the black registration border.

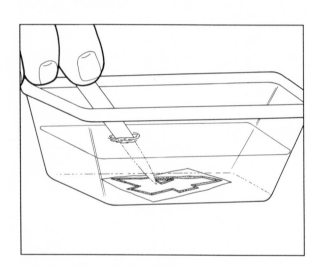

3 Soak the black registration decal in water.

Wet the red numeral four on the rooftop. This water will have no effect on the decal if it is dry.

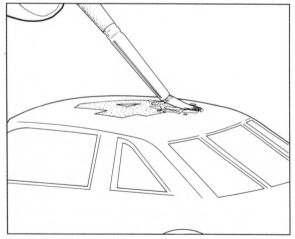

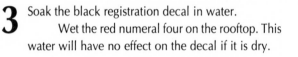

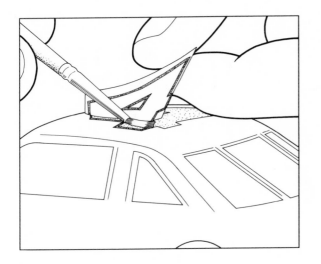

4 Follow the basic techniques for decal application (pages 50–52) and apply the black registration decal. Adjust the decal around the red numeral for precise alignment of the black lines.

Pat the decal gently with a paper towel to remove any excess water. When the decal is completely dry, apply a coat of decal-setting solution (page 52).

Repeat these steps for the remaining decals.

Remember that final application of a clear coat is a great way to protect exterior details such as weathering and decals.

The object with any of the techniques discussed is to create as realistic a model as possible. Keep in mind that they are not exclusive to cars or trucks. Try them on planes, ships, military vehicles, or even spacecraft. It's amazing how versatile a hobbyist can be by combining a selection of good hobby supplies with solid building and finishing techniques.

CHAPTER 16

DETAILING AIR AND SPACE MODELS

The great thing about building scale models is that many detailing techniques apply to other types of models. Airplanes, spacecraft, and science fiction models benefit from applications for cars, trucks, and ships. For example, using sandpaper to age a car tire is just as effective on the tire of an airplane's landing gear.

There are a few times when, because of a model's design, certain techniques become exclusive to that type of model. It wouldn't be typical to camouflage an automobile, but it's very common for military aircraft. Of course, off-road vehicles are appropriate choices for camouflage paint schemes. This illustrates how important it is for a model builder to be flexible and diverse when building and detailing scale models.

Detailing airplane, spacecraft, and science fiction models requires imagination. It is also wise to support one's imagination with research and quality reference materials. Unless it is a fantasy model, the goal is to produce as realistic a model as possible.

AIRPLANE COCKPITS

An airplane's cockpit, like the interior of a model car, screams for attention. Many kits provide a decal sheet for the instrument panel. Applying the decal directly to the panel is fine, but this gives it a one-dimensional look. Here's how to create a three-dimensional look.

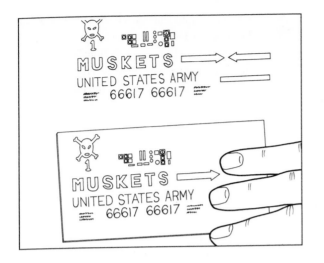

1 Make a 100-percent-size copy of the instrument panel decal.

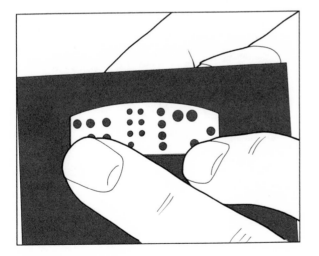

2 Either punch out or cut location holes at each dial position on the copy. The copy now becomes a template or stencil for the next step.

Lay the template over a sheet of styrene. A gauge of .010 should be fine for most airplane instrument panels. (Sheet styrene is available at most hobby retailers.)

Secure the stencil to the styrene and spray it with black paint from a can or airbrush.

3 Remove the stencil, and when the paint is dry, cut open the holes to reveal the dials. This now becomes a faceplate for the instrument panel. Then apply the instrument panel decal to the cockpit following the model kit instructions.

Measure and cut a clear piece of styrene plastic to the exact size of the panel. (Clear styrene also is available at local hobby shops. Sometimes clear plastic from food containers can substitute for stock styrene.)

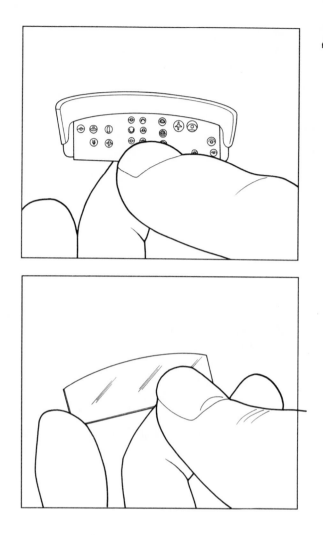

4 Using some liquid glue, attach the white faceplate to the cockpit's instrument panel (left).

Attach the clear plastic (bottom left) on top of the faceplate using some more liquid glue. The instrument panel will now have a three-dimensional look.

To make a colored faceplate, such as olive drab or gray, reverse the process for making the stencil. Instead of emphasizing holes for the dials, cut around them so the stencil exposes all areas except the dials. The stencil now produces white location holes instead of black ones after painting. Proceed from step three to complete the process.

MAKING YOUR OWN PARTS

Avid aircraft model builders will try to find old and rare model kits. It is not unlikely for these kits to be missing some, if not all, of the decals. In the event they are missing or have been damaged, there is an effective way to simulate the instrument panel without decals.

First, research the aircraft thoroughly and gather the best photographic reference materials available. Use this information to find the design and location of the instrument panel. Purchase commercially available .010-gauge stock styrene. Any size close to the dimension of .010 will work for this job. It is preferable that the styrene be molded in white. Cut the plastic according to the dimensions found in your research sources. It is necessary to combine the model's scale with some basic math to calculate the correct scale dimensions. For example, a real cockpit's dimensions for an instrument panel could be 36 inches wide, 12 inches high at the highest point, and 8 inches high at the lowest point. Divide those dimensions by the model's scale, say 1/72nd. In this

example, the model's dimensions will be .5 inches (about ½ inch) wide, .16 inch (about ⅙ inch) at the highest point, and .11 inch (about ¹⁄₁₀ inch) at the lowest one. Keep in mind these numbers are arbitrary and are for example only. Using this calculation and a scale ruler should provide accurate scale dimensions for an instrument panel, or any other part you have to make from scratch. Then follow the accompanying directions to complete the job.

Depending on scale, there are several ways to get near-perfect circles for the dials. Scales 1/48th or larger will accommodate many household items for use as a stencil. Using the research, find an item, like a hole punch, button, or even the head of a nail that equals the circumference of the dials. For scales smaller than 1/48th some math and a scale ruler will be effective guides in creating the dial circumferences freehand on the instrument panel.

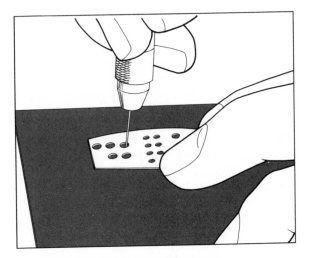

1 Spray paint the cut styrene flat (or matte) or semigloss black. Using the reference materials, find the location of the instrument dials on the panel. Scribe the dials into the plastic sheet using the tip of a pinvise or similar scribing instrument.

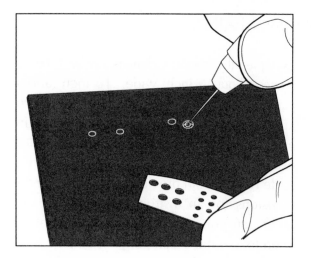

2 After scribing the dials, replicate the "ticks" or gradations on the dials. Use a scribing tool to freehand small lines carefully inside the dials to simulate these markings.

Attach the panel to the cockpit's interior and place a clear piece of styrene on top to add some visual dimension.

When completed it will be difficult for anyone to differentiate the homemade instrument panel from a set of decals that do the same job.

MAKING SEAT BELTS

Seat belts are another dominant interior feature common to airplanes. In some kits they come as part of a cockpit seat's molded detail. After painting, this detail may lose its effective impact.

Replacing this original detail with a three-dimensional seat belt is an easy addition and one that works well for cars, too!

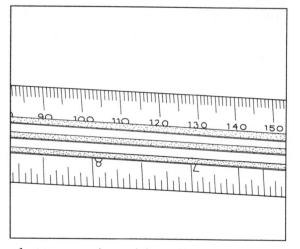

1 Measure and record the width of the molded seat belt.

Sand off the original seat belt detail from the seat. (Skip this step if the seat has no seat belt.) Be careful when sanding not to remove any leather or cloth texture details on the seat.

Cut masking tape with a hobby knife into thin strips that equal the width of the original belts. Don't worry about length until later.

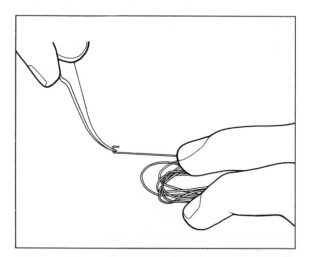

2 Get some stranded wire or electrical solder. The softer the material is the better it will work. Solder is generally the softest material available. Cut the wire or solder into small pieces.

Fold the wire over to replicate a buckle, as found in research or reference photographs. Try here to approximate the buckle's appearance and don't let the perfectionist in you hamper this process.

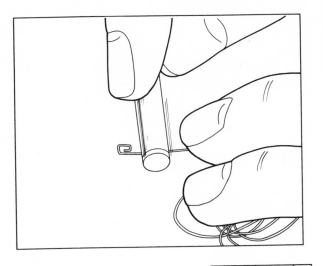

3 Use the handle of a hobby knife or similar tool and roll it over the buckle to flatten it. This step takes advantage of the solder's or thin wire's soft property.

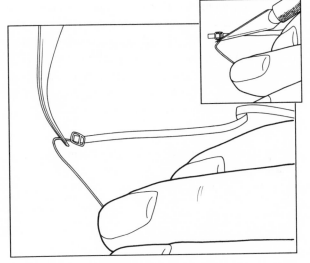

4 Loop the cut masking tape through the buckle to complete the seat belt assembly. (For color, paint the belts after cutting to assure total coverage over all edges.)

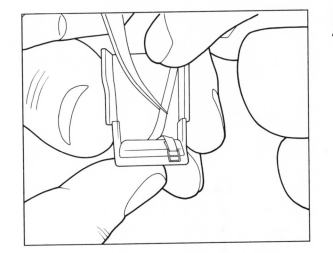

5 Drape the seat belt assembly over the seat in an irregular fashion, letting your creativity determine the final position.
    Cut off the excess length to conform with the seat's dimensions.

HELICOPTERS

Helicopter models pose some interesting challenges in creating realistic scale replicas. The presence of large areas of glass can be intimidating but also invites the challenge of recreating the tinted glass so often seen on helicopters.

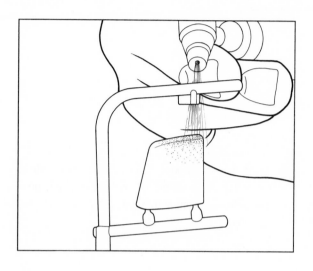

1 Using research and other reference materials, select a color for the window tint. Most often these colors will be shades of blue, green, or brown. Purchase a clear acrylic paint that matches the reference color. If the exact color is not available, you may have to mix colors. For the UH-1 Huey shown here, it was necessary to mix yellow with blue to make green paint for the tint. Prepare the paint and airbrush following standard procedures (page 47).

For ease of handling, spray paint the windows while they are still on the part's tree, removing all other pieces that need to remain clear. Paint only the back side of the part, since most tints are on the inside of windows. Allow the paint to dry.

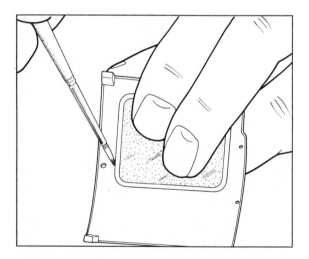

2 Install the now-tinted glass following the instructions that come with the model.

SIMULATING ENGINE VENTS

Another prevalent feature of helicopters is their engine vent screens. On larger scales these vents have a screen pattern that only simulates holes. One way to improve this detail is to use some paint and a wash to accentuate shadows where the holes should be. Although this is effective, a better method is to remove the existing vent and replace it with a more realistic material.

DeHavilland "Beaver" Bush Plane

Lockheed Vega,
"Amelia Earhart's Transatlantic Plane"

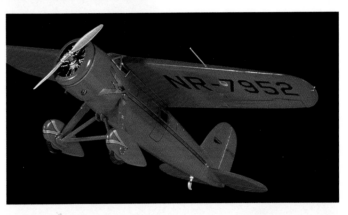

UPS DC-8 Cargo Plane

USS *Arizona*

USS *Arizona* in a diorama representing the Panama Canal

AWACS E-3 Sentry

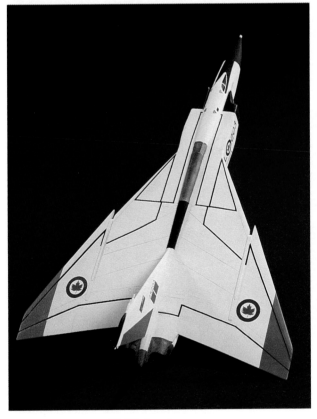

CF-105 Avro Arrow

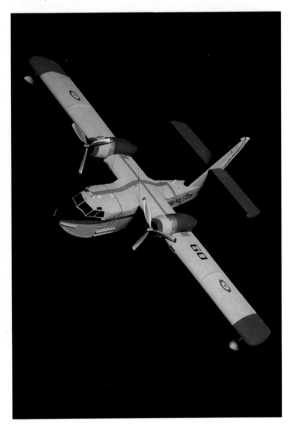

Canadair CL-215 Water Bomber

Ford F-150 Pickup Truck

Bugatti Royale

Circus Calliope Wagon

Stephenson's Rocket

Vietnam Memorial, "The Three Servicemen"

Bell "Huey" Helicopter

M24 Chaffee Tank

Boeing V-22 Osprey

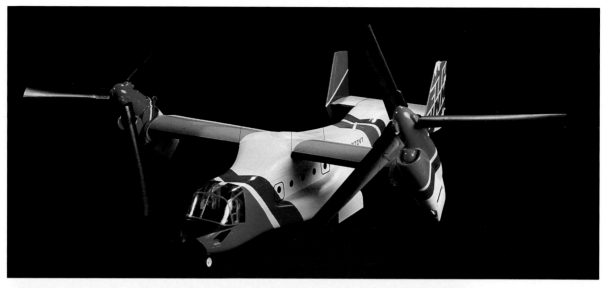

Classic 1957 Chevy

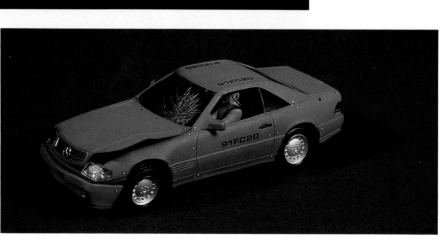

Mercedes Benz Crash Test Car

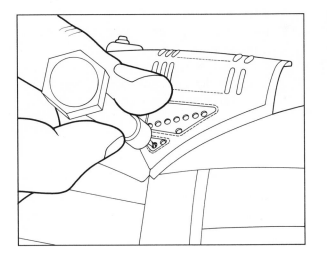

1 Drill a series of holes around the inside edge of the screen using a pin-vise or motor tool. Then drill some additional holes across the diameter of the screen to further weaken the screen area. Test the screen's integrity and add more holes if necessary.

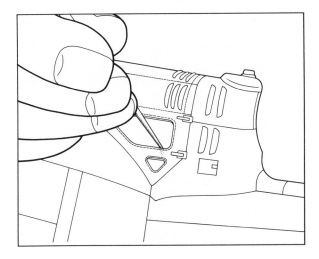

2 Carefully remove the screen area by pushing through it. Clean the rough edges and corners with a file and progressive grits of sandpaper. Make certain the edge is smooth and clean.

Select a material to use as a screen for the engine vent. Model railroad brass screen and first-aid gauze are good choices for the new vent. Since gauze is an inexpensive household item, it is usually the first choice.

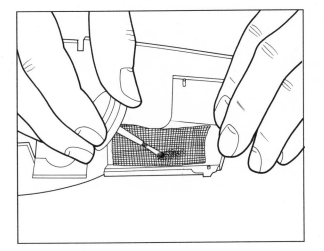

3 Cut a piece of screen material larger than the vent area. Working on the model's interior, glue the screen material in place using generous amounts of a glue that bonds dissimilar materials. If using gauze, stretch it tight without deforming its shape before gluing it in place.

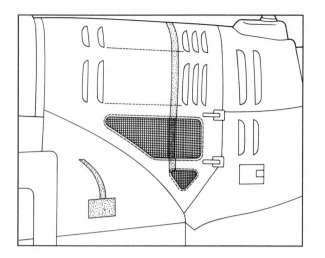

4 When the screen is dry and permanently in place, trim off the excess material from the interior of the helicopter.

Mask off the exterior around the screen vent. Spray paint the vent a flat black to create shadows and enhance the screen's appearance.

This technique will work anywhere a model has a vent area. Tank engine vents and automobile grilles are perfect places to attempt this technique.

CREATING METAL SURFACES

Commercial and military aircraft operators frequently don't paint the exterior surfaces on their planes. A high-gloss metal surface finish is one that challenges the model builder who attempts to duplicate this look with plastic. Here are some ways to produce a polished metal look.

As with cars and trucks, Bare-Metal foil is one choice for producing a metal finish on an airplane. But because there is so much area to cover, this method requires a lot of time and patience.

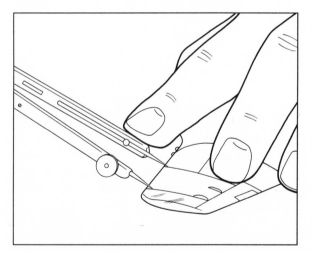

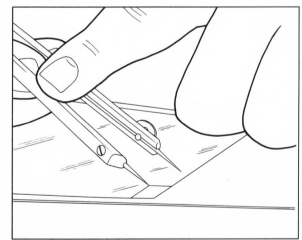

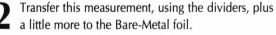

1 Get a pair of draftsman's dividers. These are essential for making precise measurements of external panel lines. A ruler can substitute, but it is prone to error when transferring measurements.

Select a panel on the aircraft and measure the length with the dividers.

2 Transfer this measurement, using the dividers, plus a little more to the Bare-Metal foil.

Repeat steps two and three for the panel's width.

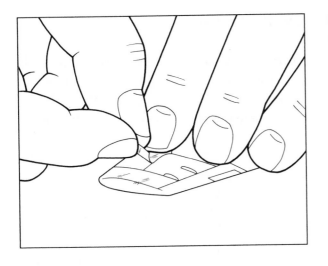

3 Make sure the model is clean and free of any exterior defects. Then, following the measurements, cut the foil and remove it from the backing paper (pages 66–67).

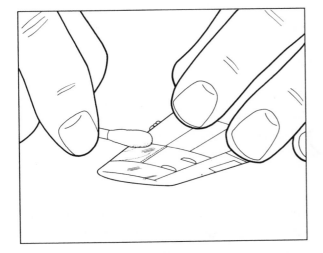

4 Place the foil over the panel of the airplane's surface. Burnish the foil so it adheres to the model, using the soft tip of a dry cotton swab (left).

Using a modeling knife, gently follow the contours of the panel line to trim off excess foil (bottom left). Remove the surplus foil and burnish the foil into the edges.

Repeat this process for the remaining panels until the airplane's exterior surface is completely covered.

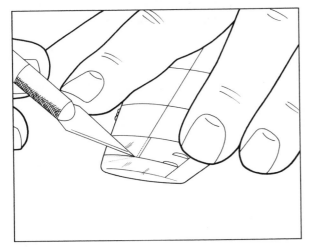

It may seem easier to jump ahead and use one large piece of foil to cover the entire wing or fuselage. Although this idea may save time, it fails to reproduce the individual panel lines that actually appear on real aircraft. The individual sheets also take advantage of the foil's natural grain pattern. Alternating the foil's direction adds another realistic detail to the aircraft's metal finish.

POLISHING IN SILVER DETAILS

A silver polishing paste is an excellent substitute for the Bare-Metal foil. The paste also will successfully duplicate a high-polish metal look. It's less tedious than the foil, and does save time.

Polishing paste contains a lacquer that al-

lows it to dry quickly. This quick-drying property is an immediate benefit for the time-conscious model builder. And since it contains so little lacquer, there is no risk of harming a model's finish.

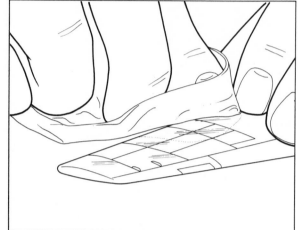

1 Apply a thin coat of paste to the model's surface with your fingertip. Keep the coats thin to reduce the chance of lumps developing on the model.

2 Take facial tissue and buff the paste to develop a look that replicates polished metal.

There are two options for securing the paste's finish to the surface. The first choice is setting the model aside to dry for two or three days to let the lacquer completely evaporate. When the lacquer evaporates, it leaves a hard,

durable surface. The second route is to spray a clear-gloss lacquer coat over the entire model. Spraying over an original lacquer job eliminates any risk of etching the model's surface.

USING LACQUER FOR SILVER FINISHES

There is still another proven method for creating a look of highly polished metal. Similar to the paste, a silver lacquer paint is available to the hobbyist. This paint also buffs to very good shine.

Before using lacquer on any model, it is important to apply a light base coat of paint that prevents the lacquer from etching the plastic. The base coat also will hide any surface imperfections and help the lacquer produce a smooth and flawless finish.

The choices for a base coat vary. If the model's surface is one color, then use a light gray. When there are other colors, such as red wing tips, or black stripes, use a reverse masking technique. The other colors will be the base coat, and the light coats won't hide any molded details.

In the following example, reverse masking is the method of choice for applying base coats to a P-51D Mustang model.

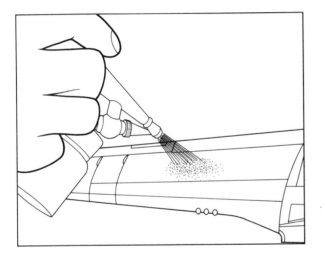

1 Use an airbrush and spray the wing or other surface with a thin coat of red lacquer, which will not harm the model's surface. When the paint dries, mask off the wing's red tip.

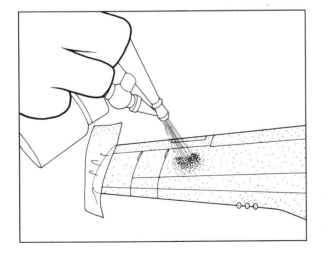

2 Now spray the wing with some black lacquer paint. Remember to apply this as thin coats of paint until proper coverage is achieved.

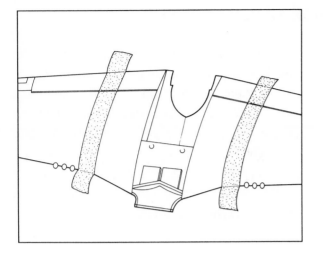

3 When the paint dries, mask off the black gun troughs and other appropriate details.

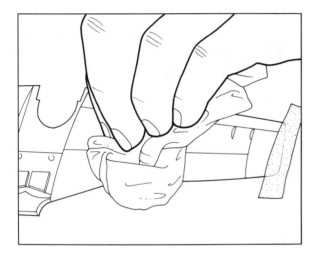

4 Using the airbrush, apply a thin coat of silver buffing lacquer. *Caution:* Silver paint is susceptible to scratching. Work with the model part on a soft, lint-free towel to reduce the chance of creating scratches.

After this final coat of paint dries, buff the silver with a soft, lint-free cloth until the desired gloss is achieved.

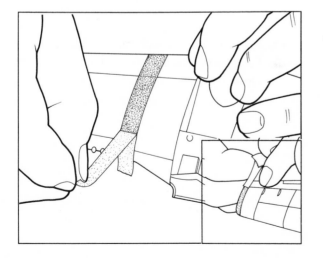

5 Remove the masking tape to reveal the red wing tips and black gun troughs. If there is any over spray, use a fine detail brush to touch up that area.

DETAILING METAL FINISHES

Many airplanes, especially war birds, have repair areas that differ in appearance from the original panels. Using different shades of silver lacquer can add even more distinctive detail to an aircraft's metal exterior.

Because of lacquer's properties, it is not possible to use masking tape. Masking tape will pull the lacquer from the model's surface and ruin its finish. There is an easy way around this problem.

Wet notebook paper is a perfect substitute for the masking tape. The wet paper, which already has a straight edge, will cling to the model because of its surface tension. Place the paper around the panel. It will stay wet long enough to airbrush a darker shade of silver on the panel.

After the paint dries, remove the paper to reveal the different shades of silver.

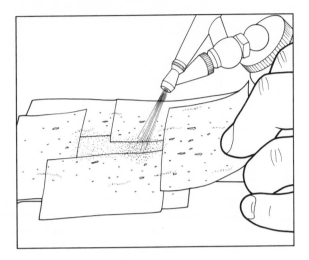

ADDING CAMOUFLAGE

Camouflage is a popular and realistic exterior finish for military aircraft. With the various branches of service, different countries, and different historic periods, selecting a style of camouflage for airplanes can be overwhelming. The most practical idea is to research various camouflage schemes as they apply to a particular aircraft.

Though it appears complicated, the application of a camouflage paint scheme can be a fun experience. The ease of the process depends largely on accurate reference photographs or instruction sheets that can include a complete pattern for a camouflage design.

An airbrush is the best tool for applying a camouflage paint scheme to a model. The superb control and spray patterns afforded by an airbrush deliver color edges that feather into each other—

an appearance prevalent in camouflage paint schemes.

Spray cans and hand painting by brush can be substituted for an airbrush. Using spray cans require masking because of their broad spray pattern. Although it cannot produce edges that feather into each other, the lines between the different colors in a camouflage pattern will be soft.

Using a paintbrush, the least desirable approach, creates hard edges between colors that do little to accurately depict a camouflage paint scheme. Thinning the paint for brush application will improve the results and minimize the risk of brush marks and covering molded details.

Here's how to get a great-looking camouflage paint scheme for any military vehicle.

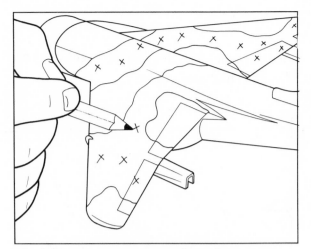 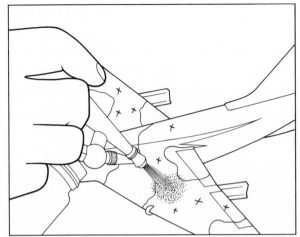

1 Select an appropriate camouflage scheme, using research or the kit instructions. In this example, a British winter scheme using gray and white paints is being prepared.

Choose a primary color from the camouflage scheme and spray paint the model with it as a light base coat. It is preferable to use the lightest color for the base coat. Let the paint dry thoroughly.

Next, take a pencil and outline the demarcation lines of the camouflage on the model by hand. Use photographs, the instructions, or the kit's box art as a reference to determine where the colors change.

After marking the lines, use the pencil and indicate the areas of one color with X's. The X on the Harrier jet, shown here, denotes the gray areas for a winter camouflage scheme.

2 Prepare the paint, in this case gray, for the airbrush. Test spray on a cardboard, checking for clogs and to adjust the spray pattern.

Carefully airbrush the X areas with the nozzle adjusted to deliver a very narrow pattern for control. Apply lighter coats of paint near the edges. Don't worry about going outside the lines. Instead of being detrimental, this will help create edges that feather into each other. Make sure that the paint completely covers the pencil marks.

After painting all the X areas gray, the winter camouflage scheme is complete.

Note: Not enough can be said about how research can produce excellent results. It is the best way to develop distinctive designs and finishes for any scale model. It can be what distinguishes one model from another in a competition or display.

REINSTATING PANEL LINES

Commercial and military aircraft models pose an interesting problem. During construction and preparation for painting, it is easy to inadvertently remove molded panel line details. This is espe-cially true on the fuselage after using putty and sanding to remove the seam line (page 34). Here's how to restore those important surface details.

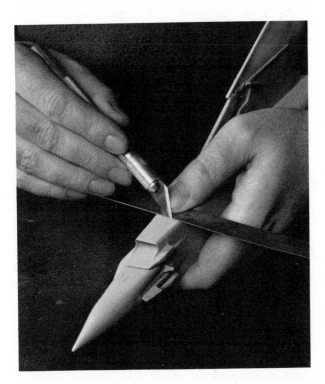

Calculate the locations of the missing panel lines. A safe way to do this is by measuring the distance between these details before sanding and making a note of the distances between them on the model's part. Another method is to use unobscured line details to find the precise locations. In the unlikely event that all the lines disappear, estimate their approximate locations using the kit's box art or reference photographs as a visual guide. Lightly mark location points on the model for panel lines.

Get a hobby knife and a steel ruler. A similar sharp instrument, professional scribing tool, and flexible straightedge will also work for this job.

Line a flexible straightedge ruler up to the location points. Use the reverse side of the hobby knife's blade and slowly follow the straightedge to restore the panel line details. The reverse side of the blade has the effect of scribing the plastic and at the same time pulling away the excess plastic from the model's surface in small curls. The sharp side of the blade would cut into the plastic, creating an undesirable effect.

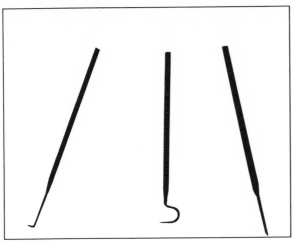

A good substitute for the hobby knife is a dental pick for cleaning between teeth. This tool works exactly like the back edge of the hobby knife blade but without the risk of accidentally cutting into the plastic.

TRANSPLANTING PARTS

An airplane's design changes very little over time, and it evolves slowly with onboard technical improvements and occasionally some modest external modifications, such as engine upgrades. Updating a model airplane kit can be done the same way.

The most common techniques for these modifications use after-market parts or *kit bashing*. Kit bashing means transplanting parts from one model, usually of similar scale, to another.

It's best to make the decision to upgrade, or change a kit, before building it. After constructing a model, changes become difficult to implement successfully.

For the Canadair CL-215 model depicted here, a decision was made to replace the original piston engines with the new turbo versions found on the CL-215T. Making any modification depends on the design, scale, complexity of the model kit, availability of replacement parts, and desired changes.

The decision to make changes comes only after knowing how to make them successfully.

Select the upgrade parts from an appropriate model kit. A similar scale Dehavilland Dash 8 model kit contains the new turbo engines we want for the CL-215 shown here. Before bashing a kit, check your spare-parts box first. It's possible to find suitable parts for many modifications without having to buy another model kit.

Remove the engine nacelles from the Dash 8 kit and assemble them following the kit instructions.

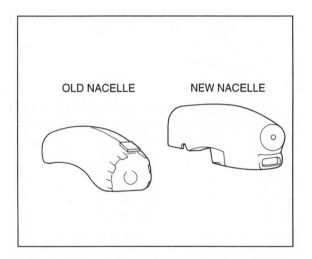

OLD NACELLE   NEW NACELLE

Comparing the turbo engine with the original piston version reveals the need to modify the wings so they can accept the new engine nacelles. It is simpler to modify the flat wing surfaces rather than the curved surfaces of the engine nacelles.

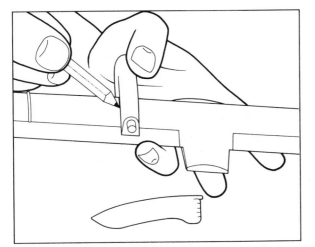

1 The CL-215's wing comes as a solid piece. Close examination shows that the original nacelle wraps around the wing for assembly. The new turbo engine nacelle cannot do this. Place the new nacelle on the wing's surface and use a pencil to mark the outside dimensions.

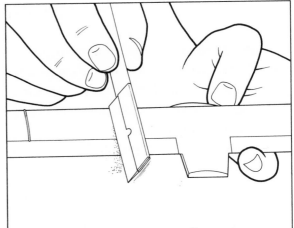

2 Carefully cut along the outline using a razor saw or similar tool to remove that wing's surface area. Clean and smooth the edges with a file and sandpaper.

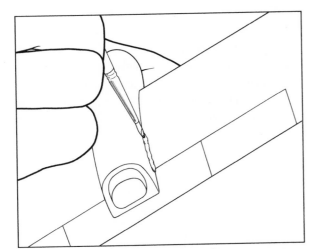

3 Glue the new engine nacelle into place on the wing surface. Fill any seams or gaps with putty. Finish these areas following the steps for filling seams. This step will help the new nacelle assembly look like it is an original model part. Repeat these steps for the remaining engine(s).

Making modifications or upgrades to model kits is a lesson in problem solving. Each model kit will challenge the builder to be inventive and creative in removing and adding parts to complete changes. By using aftermarket parts and kit bashing, the model builder confronts these challenges successfully.

AIRPLANE WINDOWS

Commercial airliners present special problems because there are numerous cockpit and passenger windows to contend with. With so many clear pieces, installation is time-consuming, and masking before painting is tedious.

One way to reduce assembly time is to install clear cockpit and passenger windows from the inside of the model. This eliminates the need to cut around individual panes, especially in the passenger area.

Here's how to save time and successfully mask all the windows for painting.

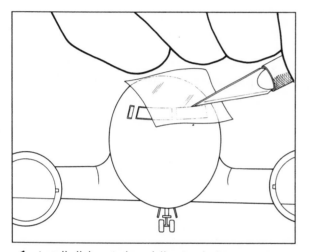

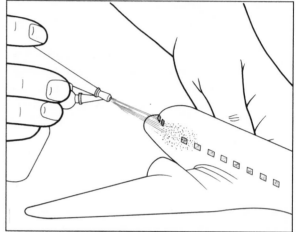

1 Install all the windows following the kit instructions. If you can, install the windows from the inside to save time. Only deviate from the kit instructions if this does not impede any of the other steps.

Mask all the window areas using clear, or frost, cellophane tape. Regular masking tape should not be substituted for cellophane tape because it is essential that the tape be transparent.

The clear cellophane should reveal all the exterior fuselage components, such as window posts, that need painting. Install a new, sharp blade in a hobby knife. Take the hobby knife and gently scribe along the sides of the window posts and around the window exteriors. It takes little, if any, pressure to make these cuts with a fresh blade, but too much force will cut too deeply into the model's plastic.

Carefully remove the tape from around the windows and the post areas. Secure all remaining cellophane edges to the airplane's fuselage. The aircraft is now ready for painting.

2 Paint the fuselage a suitable color and set it aside to dry. After removing the cellophane masking, the plane will have clear windows, with the areas between the windows and the posts matching the fuselage color.

IMPROVING DETAILS

Frequently, the model builder wants to make minor changes to a model to produce a more authentic operating appearance. Basic alterations to the ailerons, elevators, and rudder will help create more authentic-looking airplane models. Before undertaking these enhancements, it is important to understand how flight-control surfaces, such as those on wings, operate. Some minimal research will provide all the answers and assure accurate changes.

Here's how to add life to a plane by moving the ailerons into a candid position.

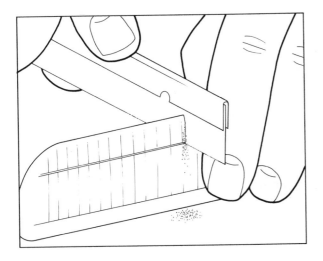

1 Get a hobby knife and a razor saw. Identify the position of the ailerons, or other control surfaces, on the model. Most airplanes will have some type of molded detail to differentiate these controls from other surface areas. On the Stearman PT-17, the aileron detail is very prominent.

Work on the bottom of the wing surface, using a razor saw to cut into the wing. Make this cut perpendicular to the wing's trailing edge. Follow the scribe lines until reaching the horizontal line that also creates the aileron detail.

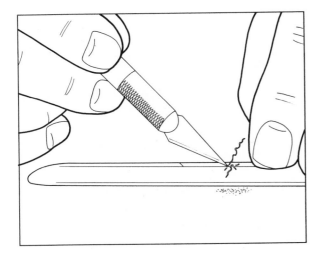

2 Now use the sharp edge of a hobby knife blade and cut through the horizontal line of the aileron. Clean the edges of the wing and aileron with a file and sandpaper. The aileron now becomes a separate part that can be attached to the model in either an up or down position. Gluing it in an upward configuration means the other aileron should be in a downward position. That is how ailerons work on real airplanes.

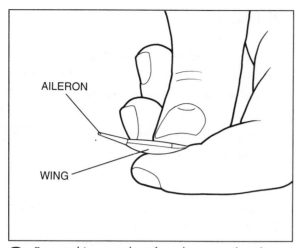

AILERON

WING

3 Repeat this procedure for other control surfaces, paying close attention to how they function and operate.

The technique described here is particularly effective for displaying airplanes in flight. On the ground, control surfaces change position as pilots conduct preflight checks before takeoff.

This technique is also great for scale figures. Many military model kits will come with figures that are positioned inside or outside a model. Moving and adjusting the head or arms results in a candid appearance that adds life to otherwise lifeless figures.

PAINTING STRIPES

For many model builders, the goal is to replicate a vehicle or aircraft that typically looks like the ones seen in a particular region or area, with the same markings and coloration. There are two ways to reach this objective. The first, as mentioned before, is to purchase after-market decals from mail order catalogues (page 79). The other option is to manufacture an original set of exterior details using paint and homemade decals.

The key to adopting the second option is to have accurate visual information about a model's prototype. If it is not possible to take photographs of the prototype, you'll have to write to manufacturers or owners. Most will respond with pictures and additional information that are useful in accurately detailing a model. Address inquiries to the attention of the company's public information office.

Let's begin with a simple technique for making stripes.

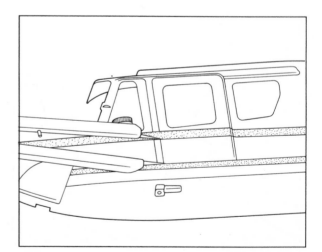

1 Use reference materials and choose the appropriate color(s) for the stripe. First paint the entire model this color, then set it aside to dry for a minimum of twenty-four hours.

Refer back to your research materials and calculate the length and width of the stripe(s). An easy way to estimate measurements is to use visual reference points, such as a door hinge and window, that appear on both the prototype and its model.

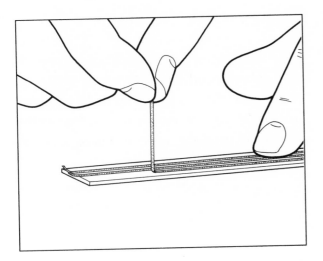

2 Transfer the length to masking tape and trim it to the precise measurement, making sure that the strips are thin enough to easily conform to any compound curves on the model.

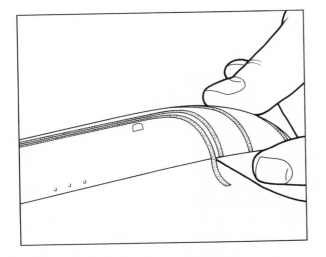

3 Place the thin strips of masking tape on the model over the location where you want the stripe to appear, paying close attention to the width. Burnish the edges of the tape securely to the model's surface, using the tip of a dry cotton swab.

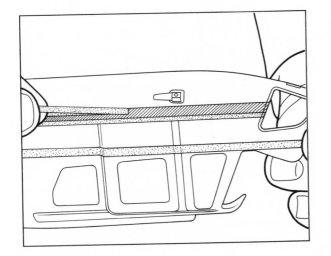

4 Double-check to confirm that the tape wraps around all curves, especially the fuselage on an aircraft model.

Paint the model its primary exterior color using an airbrush or spray can. Set the model aside to dry for at least twenty-four hours.

When the model is thoroughly dry, remove the masking tape to reveal a good clean stripe. This reverse-masking technique is also effective in producing similar exterior details on other types of models.

MAKING DECALS

When a model like the Lifeflight helicopter shown here has complex exterior color schemes, it is sometimes necessary to make decals. Attempting to paint so much detail can often cover up molded details and ruin a model's exterior appearance. Your best bet is to make these details out of decals.

Most quality hobby shops will stock plain and colored decal sheets. If not, try looking in trade publications to locate mail order catalogue companies that offer these materials. Estimate the amount of decal the model will need, and purchase a little extra.

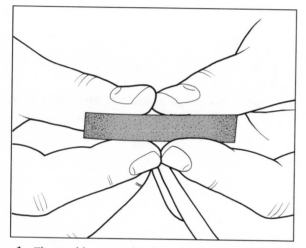

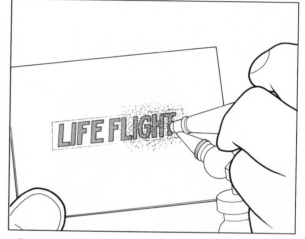

1 Thoroughly researching your subject will help in choosing the correct colors to finish exterior details. In this example, the need is for a burgundy background and silver corporate logo.

Calculate the background dimensions and cut a plain sheet of decal paper to size. Secure the decal paper to stiff card stock and spray paint it the correct color. Set the decal aside to dry.

2 The process now becomes a bit more involved. It is essential to have a quality visual reference of the prototype to successfully complete the next steps.

Make a photocopy of the photograph at a copy center or library. Enlarge or reduce your picture reference so it most accurately reflects the dimensions of the model's scale. Use basic math to calculate the dimensions, or simply try different size percentages on the photocopy machine. Remember, a reasonable ballpark figure should work fine for this application.

After getting the photocopy close to size, cut it out to make a stencil. Place and secure the lettering or logo pattern stencil on top of the burgundy background decal sheet.

Using the correct color—for the Lifeflight helicopter shown here it is silver—spray paint the background over the stencil. Set it aside to dry thoroughly, preferably overnight.

3 Remove the stencil to reveal a two-color decal incorporating a color background and corporate logo.

4 Apply the decal to the precise location using the application techniques in Chapter 12.

With access to good reference photographs and copy machines, it is not too difficult to replicate local or regional logos. The combination of these outside additions with other exterior and interior details will surely produce aviation and spacecraft models that look almost exactly like their prototypes. Be imaginative and willing to try new things and the results will be rewarding.

CHAPTER 17

DETAILING MILITARY VEHICLES AND ARMOR

Other than automobiles, no category offers a larger selection than military model kits. The choices include aircraft, armored vehicles, and ships. This broad variety makes military model building the most popular choice among hobbyists. The diversity also creates the greatest versatility with construction and finishing techniques.

The ability to replicate historical as well as modern military equipment relies on good model kits, solid research, and a combination of construction and detailing techniques. A good model kit includes finishing ideas, such as camouflage schemes, extra "add on" parts, and some background data about the prototype. Additional research materials supply conclusive visual materials to aid the model-building process.

Many military kits, unlike other models, contain optional detailing parts. Adding these parts to the model is the first step in creating a more realistic scale replica. Combining these with different assembly, painting, and finishing techniques also helps to depict the appearance of a military vehicle more accurately.

ANTENNAS

Beyond what the kit provides, there are several ways to add details to armored vehicles. One simple addition to an armor vehicle is a realistic whip antenna. This distinctive exterior detail appears on Jeeps, tanks, and other armored vehicles.

Some model kits may provide a detail part such as the antenna. When this piece is molded, the antenna often turns out too thick for its scale. Model builders often refer to this characteristic as "heavy" detail. This happens when parts appear larger than scale and detract from the model's appearance.

Here are two ways to replace a kit's original antenna with materials that more closely match the model's scale.

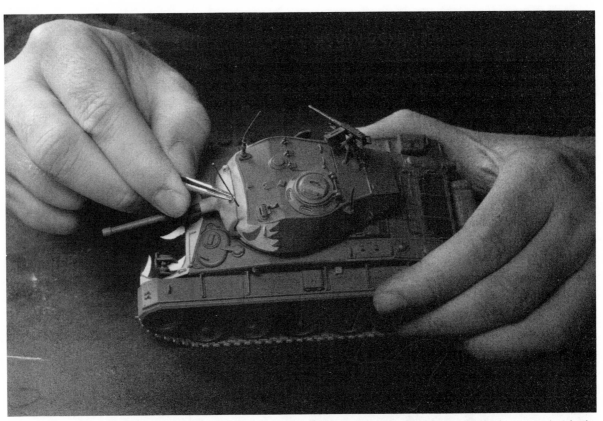

Purchase music wire from a local hobby retailer. Music wire is a common term that defines finely drawn steel rod. The rod is flexible and comes in different diameters. Model builders frequently use it for axles, railings, and other suitable applications. Cut the wire using only metal wire cutters. The steel rod will permanently damage scissors or knives. Calculate the correct diameter by comparing the wire to the hole where the antennae attaches to the model.

Refer to research materials or use the original antenna as a measure and cut the wire to the correct length. Be careful, because the wire's tension can cause it to spring unexpectedly and become a harmful flying object.

Use a cyanoacrylate glue to bond the wire to the model. Remember that one of the "super" glues or white glue is effective for bonding dissimilar materials.

Paint the antenna to blend with the vehicle's camouflage, or leave it the original silver if appropriate. Brush painting is the best choice for such a small detail part.

STRETCHING SPRUE

The next approach for making an antenna is by stretching sprue. This technique is more economical and produces a part made from the kit's original plastic.

Successfully stretching sprue takes a combination of technique and finesse. It requires a small open flame from a candle and unpainted, raw plastic from the model kit. Use enough sprue to keep fingers a safe distance from the candle's flame.

Remove all flammable materials from the area before beginning this technique. Children require close supervision during this procedure.

Here's how to successfully stretch sprue.

1 Get the piece of sprue ready and light a candle. Hold the sprue above the open flame, carefully rotating it between your fingers for even heating.

2 As the plastic heats, it can be pulled apart to create a thin wirelike material.

This is where the finesse comes in. Besides experience, there is no precise way to know when to stretch the sprue. It is strictly a judgment call that changes with each piece of sprue.

The challenges are to know when it's soft enough, to keep it from burning, and to stretch the piece without breaking it apart. It also is necessary to be able to visually approximate the diameter of the antenna. Thankfully, there is plenty of extra plastic in the model kit to practice with!

3 After successfully stretching the sprue, set it on a worktable to cool and harden. Because the plastic is so thin, it doesn't take very long for this to happen.

Cut the sprue to the antenna's correct length. Attach the antenna to the model using the appropriate glue or cement. In the event the sprue's diameter is just slightly too wide, use a hobby knife and carefully trim excess plastic from one end of the antenna. Frequently check the diameter until it fits firmly into the location hole.

WELD LINES

Exterior features unique to armored military vehicles are weld lines. The molding process produces perfectly smooth seam lines between exterior components. This is not often an accurate replication of an armored vehicle's rough exterior construction, as weld beads are typically irregular in shape. Reference photographs confirm that pieces of armor have rough welds along seams that are a dominant exterior detail. Here are two ways to duplicate this appearance.

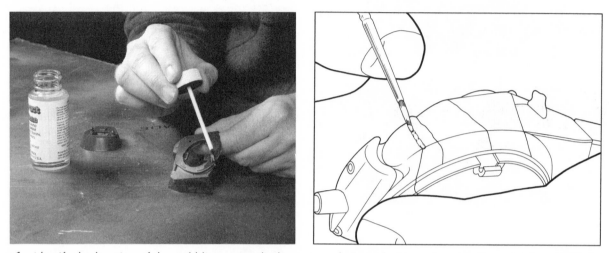

1 Identify the location of the weld line, using the box art or photographs as a reference. The turret is a common location for such an effect. Run some extra solvent along the edges where the two pieces join to make the seam. The right glue for the job is a liquid cement that reacts with and melts the plastic. The extra glue will cause the plastic to soften excessively. Another method is to lay a bead of white glue along seams.

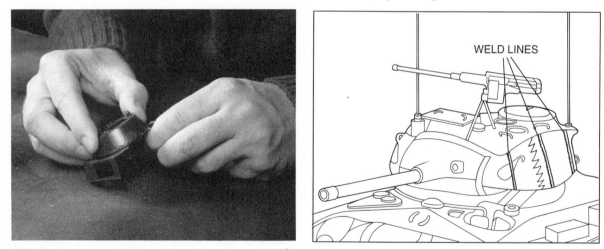

2 Join the pieces, following the model kit's instructions, allowing the extra glue to ooze out between the seam line. Set the part aside to dry.

After you have completed all construction and finishing steps, the model should have an irregular weld line around the seam.

USING WHITE GLUE TO CREATE WELDS

Some model builders may find the weld line still looks too smooth. Another method uses white glue as a filler to produce a weld line.

First assemble the model parts using the correct liquid cement, and set the assembly aside to dry. Then take the white glue and lay a bead directly around the original seam line. Depending on the model's scale, apply the glue straight from the bottle, with the toothpick and palette technique (page 19), or a fine paintbrush.

Since the white glue shrinks, it is often necessary to lay as many as three beads of glue around the seam. This will assure an accurate production of a rough weld. Apply the final bead in an irregular pattern to enhance the look of a rough weld line. After the glue dries, paint the model its appropriate color.

MODIFYING VEHICLE SUSPENSIONS

An interesting way to construct military armored vehicles is with a candid appearance. One method is to position the tracks of these vehicles to look as if they are riding over an irregular surface or obstacle. The model's suspension can be made to look even more realistic with a few modifications.

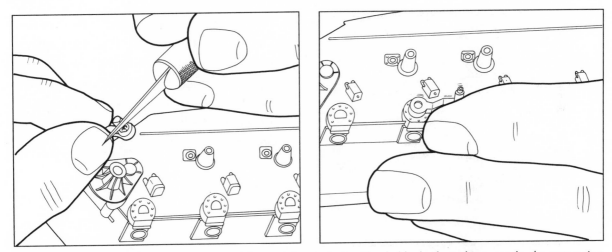

1 Identify the pin on the suspension arm of the model and trim it with a hobby knife. In this example, the suspension piece comes shaped as a letter *D*. The knife is used to round off the corners of the pin so that it can move. The key, no matter what shape pin, is to round it off for ease of movement.

Connect the suspension arm to the road wheel following the assembly instructions.

Depending on location and effect, place the suspension arm in an up or down position. The Chaffee tank model here is in an up configuration that simulates the tank running over a log in a diorama display.

The modification is not yet complete. The pulling up of the suspension's arm should force the shock absorber to change shape. The scale model's absorber looks just like a real one; it has a smaller tube entering a larger one. The difference is the kit shock absorber doesn't compress and only comes in a flat position. Here's how to adjust the shock absorber so it looks operational.

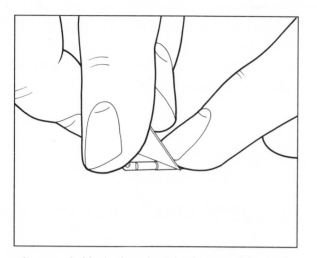

1 Use a hobby knife and cut the thin part of the shock absorber from the thick end.

2 Remove an appropriate amount of the thin end with a hobby knife. Discard the excess and attach the remaining piece back on to the thick end. This compresses the shock and simulates a down force. *Note:* Never trim the thin tube without removing it from the thick end first. The top of the thin tube has an arm that is part of the suspension. You must remove any material above the base to preserve the arm.

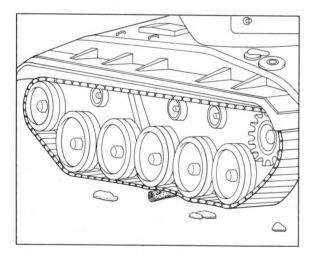

3 Attach the shock absorber to the suspension following the model's instructions. The suspension and shock assembly now looks as if it is rolling over an obstacle.

The suspension and shock absorber technique is most effective in a diorama display. A diorama is a miniature scene, exterior or interior, that places a model in one of its natural environments. This approach greatly enhances a model's presentation. Techniques for building dioramas appear in Chapter 19.

PAINTING ON CAMOUFLAGE

Almost all military armor vehicles employ camouflage to blend in with natural surroundings. One approach is to duplicate the camouflage application technique for aircraft (pages 95–96). It may be easier though, because of armor's sharp corners and crevices, to forgo the pencil marks and freehand the effect with an airbrush. Irregular surfaces also make it nearly impossible to successfully apply camouflage schemes with a brush.

Here's the best approach for applying camouflage to armor vehicles.

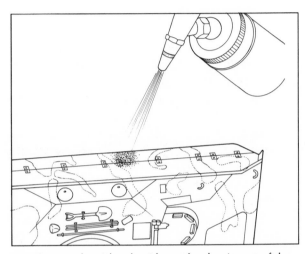

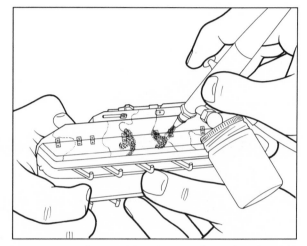

1 Prepare the airbrush with a color that is part of the camouflage paint scheme. Before beginning, test the airbrush for clogs and to ensure the correct spray pattern, which is wide for this application, and paint the entire model. Set it aside to dry overnight or follow the paint's recommended drying time.

Load the airbrush with the next camouflage color—typically, it's olive drab. Test for clogs again and adjust for a narrow spray pattern.

Paint the model, using photographs, box art, or kit instructions to develop the camouflage scheme. It is important to move slowly around the model to assure that the paint enters every nook and cranny on the tank's exterior.

2 Repeat this procedure for any other colors the camouflage scheme calls for. Remember, camouflage designs are erratic with no two vehicles ever completely alike in any scheme. This leaves room for error even when following detailed reference photographs.

ENGINE VENTS

Another exterior detail begging for special attention is an engine vent. Model companies frequently mold the grillwork in a solid honeycomb pattern. This design, similar to the real thing, causes shadows and dark areas to occur within the grille. Here's how to effectively accentuate the engine vent after applying a camouflage scheme or other exterior finish.

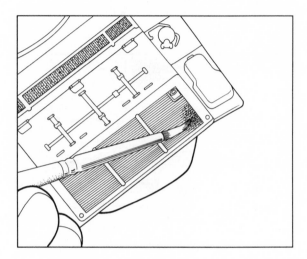

Prepare a black wash using acrylic paint, enamel paint, or india ink (page 68). Remember that an enamel wash will be permanent. It is preferable to use either an acrylic or india ink solution for this wash technique. Acrylic and india ink washes are very similar. They are easy to work with, and clean up with little trouble. In this example, the wash is an acrylic water-based solution.

Make a wash mixture using about 60 to 70 percent of the correct thinner. Add a drop or two of dishwashing detergent to reduce the surface tension of the water. Keep in mind that this is only a guideline, not a precise formula. Test the wash solution on the bottom of the model until you are happy with the results.

Apply the wash to the grille area with a paintbrush. The wash solution naturally flows into the shallow regions to create dark and shadowy areas. Repeat this technique for any other surface details needing a similar effect.

Remove any excess wash with a cotton swab. Dampen the tip with the appropriate thinner, water, or isopropyl alcohol. Rub the cotton swab's tip gently across the vent area, or other surface detail, to clean off the extra wash mixture.

Another interesting way to detail the engine vent is by employing the same technique used for the model UH-1 Huey helicopter (pages 88–90). Replacing the vent with a realistic screen material can improve the model's authenticity. Model-railroad brass screen is the best choice for armored vehicles. Since these models tend to come in smaller scales, the medical gauze used for the helicopter's grille is generally too large for this application.

CAMOUFLAGE NETTING

A final camouflage technique uses a net to cover the tank within its surroundings. Here's how to make a camouflage net if the model kit does not come with one or if it isn't realistic enough.

1 At a fabric center, find some netting that is close to the same scale as your model. Don't worry about being exact; the tank or armor to be covered should be slightly visible beneath the netting. Cut the netting with scissors to a size that allows it to drape completely over the model.

2 Use an airbrush to spray paint a camouflage scheme, or a color that matches the environment (for example, a light shade of tan for a desert setting) on the net. Paint both sides of the net and set it aside to dry overnight.

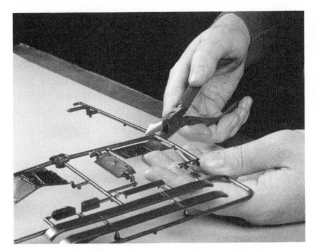

3 Take some long pieces of sprue from the part's tree and cut them into different lengths to make support posts for the net.

4 Paint the posts a color that blends with the camouflage scheme, such as olive drab.

In the field, it's likely these posts would come from natural materials such as tree limbs.

Here's how to transform the plastic sprue into something that simulates wood.

5 Use a hobby knife and the adzing technique (page 74) to form irregular shapes with the plastic.

Carefully use the back edge of the knife's blade to scribe some small vertical lines into the posts. These lines will simulate the look of wood grain.

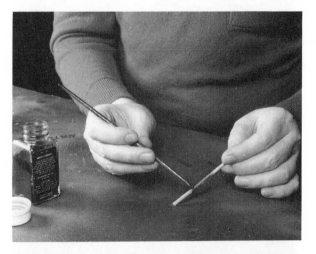

6 Paint the posts with a brush using an appropriate shade of brown. Set them aside to dry.

Use the same wash solution from the engine vent technique to accentuate the lines and improve the simulation of wood grain texture.

7 When everything is thoroughly dry, attach the posts to the base of the diorama around the armored vehicle. Place the net over the posts and attach it with some cyanoacrylate glue, or with white glue for a less permanent bond.

The netting adds another layer of camouflage and improves the model's three-dimensional presentation.

INDIVIDUALIZING ARMORED VEHICLES

Tank and armored vehicle commanders, like fighter pilots, took great pride in their machines. Many did, and still do, create a unique visual identity combining special paint jobs with a camouflage scheme. Painting from reference photographs or after-market decals are the perfect ways to give any armor piece an individual identity.

Don't lose heart when a choice is not available as an after-market decal. Use the reverse masking and homemade decal techniques found in Chapter 12 to effectively replicate a special paint scheme. With good reference photographs and an understanding of scale, anything is possible.

PAINTING SMALL PARTS

Military model kits, especially armor, contain many small parts. Painting these pieces with the base color while they are still on the tree produces the best results. A small challenge arises with this technique for wheels, tires, and hubs that need to be painted three different colors.

Here's how to add two colors to the entire wheel assembly while maintaining original colors where necessary.

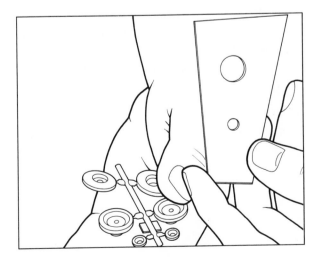

1 Use a detail brush (a number 3/0 is perfect) and paint all the tires black. Set them aside to dry.

Once the wheel assembly is completely dry, make a template, or stencil, for the hub. (This step can also occur before any painting takes place.)

Measure the wheel's hub and use those dimensions to draw it on a three- by five-inch index card, or any similar paper stock.

Take a hobby knife and cut a hole in the index card to expose the hub. The card now becomes a stencil for the wheel's hub.

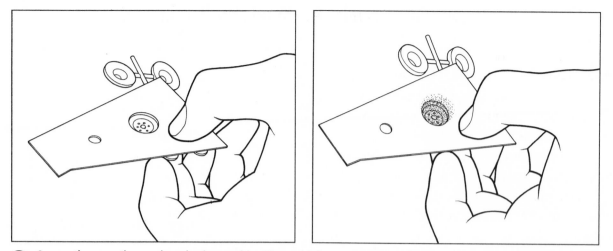

2 Secure the stencil over the wheel assembly. Then add the appropriate color to an airbrush (or another suitable delivery system) and paint the wheel's hub. Repeat these steps for each wheel assembly. A stencil is the perfect tool for applying multicolored paint schemes to small parts from any model kit.

REVERSE MASKING WITH SHIPS

Ships are another popular model-building subject for the military enthusiast. Some historical vessels have interesting paint schemes that can be quite a challenge to duplicate successfully. Reverse masking works well in meeting this challenge.

A great example of this technique is demonstrated on the USS *Yorktown*'s pre–World War II flight deck. Historical photographs show that the deck was painted in three colors: gray, brown, and yellow. The predominant color is brown, with a small gray edge along the hull, and thin yellow stripes on the deck.

Traditional painting methods call for an initial application of the brown color. Following this step, the model builder masks the model once for the gray lines and once for the yellow stripes. But this can cause some problems.

Because brown is such a dark color, it will take several heavy coats of the gray and yellow to get total coverage. The result usually obscures molded details that are important to the model's exterior finish. With reverse masking, it becomes possible to reduce the layers of paint and preserve all the exquisite molded details.

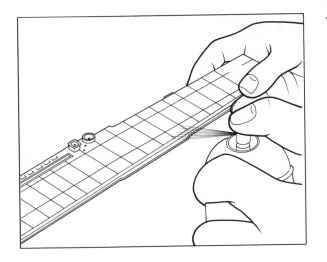

1 Paint the entire area in the lightest color. In this example, yellow is used for the deck stripes. Set the part aside to dry completely. Then cut some thin strips of masking tape to get clean edges and to help it conform around any compound curves. Mask the areas for the gray deck edges. Don't use tape for the entire process—get some notebook paper and use it to protect the remaining deck surface and the ship's hull.

Apply the next color and set it aside to dry before removing any masking material. After it dries, remove the masking material and prepare more thin strips of tape.

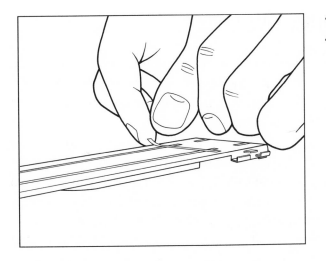

2 Use reference photographs to find the location of the yellow stripes. Make calculations or estimate the stripes' dimensions.

Cut some more masking tape to match the dimensions of the yellow stripes, and apply the tape to the deck, using the photographs as a guide. Use the remaining tape to mask the gray edges. Paint the deck with a light coat of the original color—yellow in this example—or with a clear coat. This additional light coating helps to seal the tape and prevent the next color from seeping underneath the masking medium. When using more than two colors, the clear coating is the best choice to seal the tape's edges. Set the model part aside to dry before the final application.

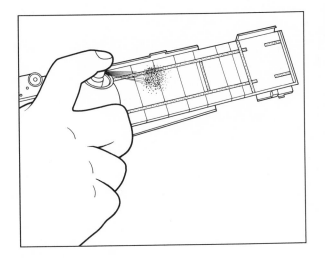

3 Prepare the brown paint using a spray can or airbrush and test spray for clogs. Completely cover the deck, and other model surfaces with the paint. Set this aside to dry overnight.

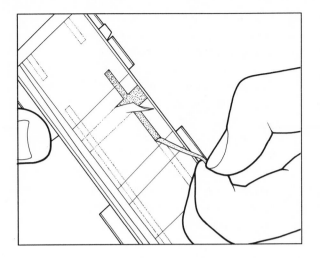

4 When the paint is thoroughly dry, remove the masking material to reveal the yellow stripes and gray deck edges.

Reverse masking is an invaluable model-building technique. The key is always to begin with the lightest color. This minimizes the total coats of paint and protects molded exterior surface details.

CREATING DISTINCTIVE EFFECTS

Military vehicles and vessels have distinctive markings that distinguish them from similar-looking nonmilitary vehicles and that distinguish vehicles from different branches of the military. Sometimes a model kit will contain decals that duplicate these markings. When they don't, it is easy to make them from scratch using research materials as a guide.

The first choice, and simplest, is to try to get some after-market decals, which are easy to apply and save time.

The other possibilities involve making either the decals or using stencils to paint on the detail. Paint is the best choice for something that has a simple design; it requires fewer materials and saves time.

The pre–World War II USS *Yorktown* uses a large black *Y* on the side of its superstructure for identification. During war, this *Y* was removed to improve the effectiveness of the ship's solid-gray camouflage. Since the original model kit was intended as a war version of the ship, the *Y* decal is absent. Here's how to restore this detail using paint.

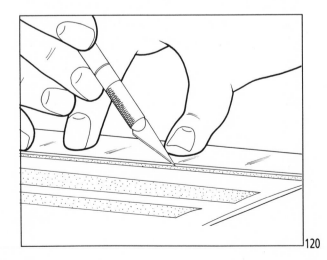

1 Use research materials and photographs to calculate the size and precise location of the *Y*. Carefully cut some masking tape to produce good, straight edges and mask off the shape you want to create on the model.

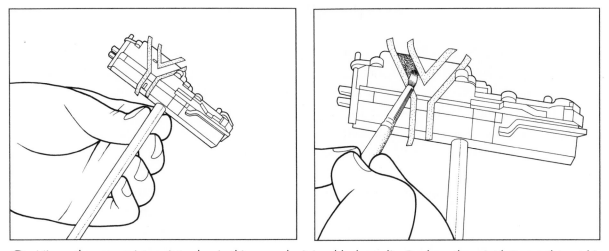

2 Mix up the appropriate paint color; in this example, it is a black acrylic. Brush on the paint between the mask's outline to create a *Y* on the super structure. The application of a clear coating before painting, as with the deck, will seal the masking tape. This, again, prevents the black paint from seeping underneath the masking medium.

Contrary to standard practice, it is best to paint with a brush for this technique. The brush is effective for small areas and saves time because there is no need for additional masking. If spray painting is preferred, then be sure to thoroughly mask the rest of the model.

Keep this technique in mind when you want to create the many simple markings that are distinguishing characteristics for a variety of military aircraft, land vehicles, and ships.

AFTER-MARKET PARTS

Military model subjects are the perfect medium for using after-market parts. Hobby shops and mail order catalogues offer an abundance of exterior detail parts. These include picks and shovels, water cans, fuel cans, camouflage netting (don't forget how to make your own), extra tracks, and much more. Using additional parts helps to enhance a model's realism and improves its visual impact.

If after-market parts are hard to find, substitute spare parts from other model kits. Many items can effectively replicate fuel cans, pipes, tools, gadgets, or other exterior details typically found on military vehicles. Pay attention to the model's scale and choose parts that are of the same or approximate size. Use your imagination in adapting parts for your purposes.

To be successful with any "add on" part, you need good research and reference materials. Photographs of military vehicles in the field and in action will show how servicemen and women use various nonissue, civilian accessories. Use your reference materials to find shapes, designs, and locations for these items. Be inventive. It's easy to combine parts and pieces to replicate accessories accurately on the real thing.

Hardworking military vehicles rarely look fresh off the assembly line. Incorporating any number of detailing and finishing techniques can distinguish models from those built following only the assembly instructions that come in a model's box.

CHAPTER 18

DETAILING MODEL SHIPS

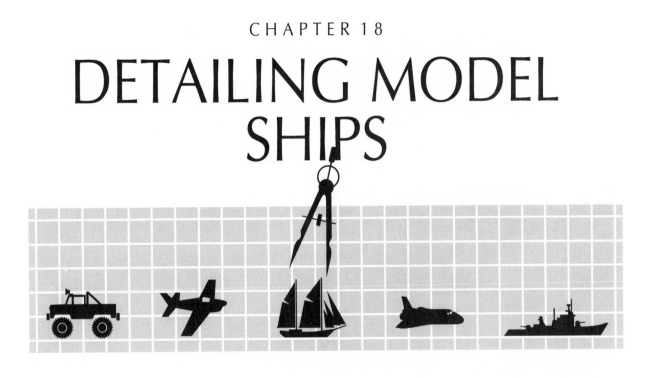

The most popular model kits given as gifts are the USS *Constitution* and models of other majestic, tall ships. For the beginner or average model builder, these kits, despite their exquisite details, can present good reasons to abandon the hobby forever because they contain a myriad of parts and a construction complexity that challenge even the most seasoned model builder. Luckily, this is not true for all ship models. There is a wide selection of commercial and military ship models perfect for developing advanced construction and finishing techniques that are needed to take on a sophisticated model like the *Constitution*. If you get a complicated gift model, set it aside until your model-building skills are up to the challenge.

Ship models share the same basic construction and painting techniques needed for cars, planes, and military vehicles. Remember that most techniques are not exclusive to any one type of model. Evaluate each situation and determine how different applications used on a variety of models can apply to the job at hand.

While model ships draw on standard modeling techniques, they have several design features that differentiate them from other types of models. Creating an accurate waterline, detailing deck surfaces, and making rigging are just some examples of how ships require some model-building techniques unique unto themselves.

A dominant exterior feature on model ships is the waterline, which shows where the hull rests above the water when fully loaded with cargo or unloaded. In yacht racing, like the America's Cup, the length of this line instead of the hull is the measurement used to classify a vessel.

CORRECTING AN INACCURATE WATERLINE

Model companies make every effort to mold in accurate waterlines. Look for this effect by examining the line and making sure it goes straight around the entire hull. (The curve of the bow or stern can cause the illusion of an ascending line.)

One common flaw is a waterline that rises at the ship's bow. Correcting this flow isn't easy, but it's necessary in producing an accurate model ship. Here's how to correct an inaccurate waterline.

1 Conduct some research and find where the waterline should be. A maritime museum is an excellent resource for this kind of information. Measure and record the distance between the top of the ship's hull and the waterline, making this measurement from the center of the ship.

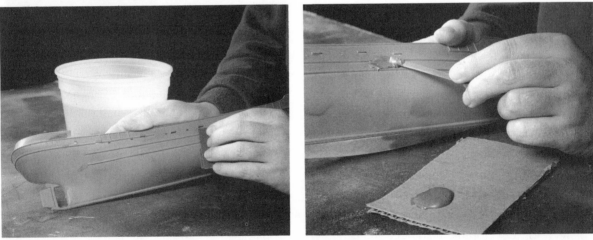

2 Remove the ship's original waterline, using one of two methods:

a) File and sand the ship's hull to remove the molded waterline detail. Remember that wet-sanding reduces the risk of damaging a model from the intense heat generated by friction.

b) Fill the waterline detail using a putty to flatten out the ship's hull. Refer to Chapter 9 for details about using putties.

Make a tool for applying a waterline to the ship's hull (see pages 125–127). This device will be versatile and work on any type of model ship. Remember, good design and background information will make this technique easier.

MAKING A WATERLINE TOOL

Here's how to make a waterline tool using simple materials. The materials needed to make a waterline tool include: a piece of ¾-inch birch plywood, a minimum of 6 by 6 inches in area; several pieces of 1-inch by 2-inch fir; D or penny nails; a ¼-by-20 carriage bolt and similar wing nut; ¼-inch and ⅜-inch washers; and a ¼-inch-thick, 3½-inch-long piece of plywood.

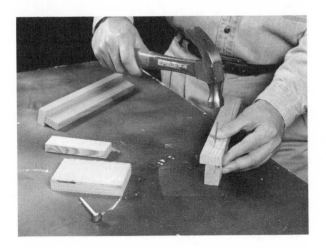

1 The base must have a truly flat surface. Use a piece of ¾-inch plywood for this purpose. Plywood resists cupping and warping better than solid stocks. It's possible to find scraps of this material around the house or at the lumberyard. Cut the plywood into a 4½-inch by 2¾-inch piece.

Cut the fir into four pieces, each 10 inches long. Cut another piece of fir 4½ inches long to cap the top of the tool.

Find the center of the face of one of the 10-inch fir pieces. Use the penny nails to attach it to another fir piece, making a T-shaped unit. Three nails should be plenty, and a little carpenter's glue will add stability. Repeat, making another T-shaped unit.

 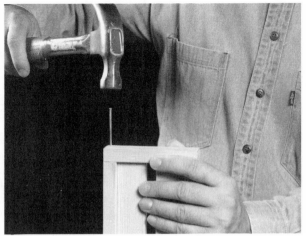

2 Align and attach the two T-shaped units to the center of the base. Leave a gap slightly larger than a pencil and face the narrow edges in.

3 Nail the cap on top of the two Ts to increase stability.

4 Make the channel block using a ¼-inch-thick, 3½-inch-long piece of plywood. Make sure the width allows the block to move freely in the tool's channel.

Drill one hole to accept the diameter of a pencil, and another hole to accept the ¼-by-20 carriage bolt. Make sure there is room between the holes to accommodate both the pencil and the carriage bolt's wing nut.

Because wood is soft, it is possible for the channel block washer to create indentations. These deformations can result in inaccuracies when marking a hull's waterline. Avoid problems by being careful not to overtighten the wing nut, or by adding a metal leading edge to the tool to protect the wood.

5 Attach the block to the tool using the carriage bolt, washers, and wing nut. Insert the pencil and loosen the bolt assembly to adjust the waterline position as needed. Mark the hull carefully to indicate the new, and correct, waterline.

USING THE WATERLINE TOOL

After removing the old waterline and preparing the ship's hull, use the tool you made to finish the job.

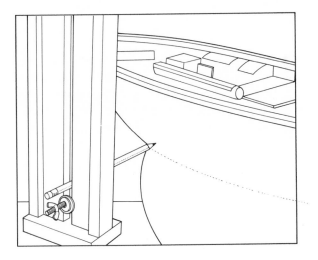

Place the hull on a base or another platform that assures it is perfectly level. Use your research and calculations to determine the height of the ship's waterline. To help with this process, measure from the top of the hull. Another option is to use the measurement from step one on page 124. Adjust the tool so the pencil lines up where you determine the waterline to fall on the side of the hull. Use the tool to carefully guide the pencil along the hull to mark the new waterline. Be patient and move slowly to avoid errors. Use this technique to apply a new waterline to each side of the hull.

USING MASKING TAPE ON IRREGULAR SURFACES

Besides requiring an accurate waterline, a ship's hull poses other challenges. The compound curves at the bow and stern make it difficult to apply masking tape to the hull. Using tape peeled directly off the spool will often not work. The width and lack of a clean edge hamper the masking process.

However, cutting masking tape on a hard surface will aid in producing an effective masking medium. The best surface for this task is a twelve-inch-square pane of glass. A scrap piece of glass is available from a local glass shop. Ask the dealer to round off the edges to make it safer to handle. You can also apply some heavy tape, such as electrical gaffer tape, to cover the sharp edges. With an adequate cutting surface, you can now prepare the hull for painting.

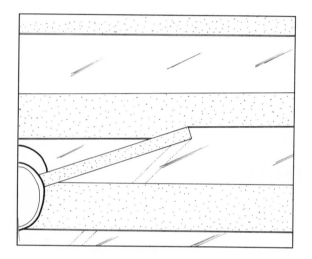

1 Cut the masking tape on the glass surface into strips that are approximately 1/8-inch wide. This width helps the tape conform to the compound curves of the bow and stern.

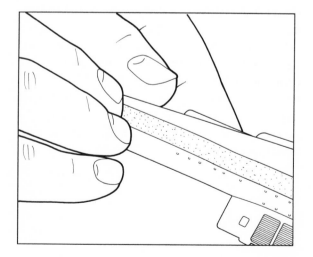

2 Apply the tape to the hull following the existing waterline or the one you created. When applying tape to the compound curves, make sure that the tape lies completely flat on the model's surface. Any irregularities will allow paint to seep underneath the tape.

Mask the remaining hull area up to the waterline color.

MASKING LARGE AREAS

Using masking tape to cover the remaining hull wastes tape and time. The best way to mask large areas is with ordinary paper, some masking tape, and cellophane tape. Here's a quick and effective way to protect large surface areas.

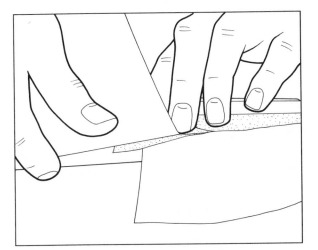

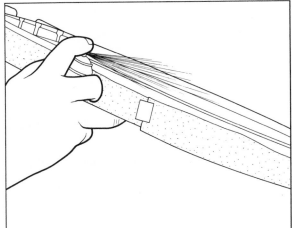

1 Cut ordinary notebook paper or stationery into manageable sizes. Newspaper is not suitable because the ink can seep through the paper to the model's surface.

    Apply the paper to the hull with masking tape, following the edge of the waterline mask. A perfectly straight edge is not necessary, because it overlaps the trimmed masking tape. Completely cover the hull, letting each piece of paper overlap by one inch.

    It is essential that all overlapping pieces of paper are secured to each other. Skipping this step will allow the force of the spray to lift up any loose edges of paper. When this happens, paint will seep underneath the mask and onto the model's surface.

    Take the cellophane tape and tape down each edge of paper where it overlaps.

2 Select the correct paint color and prepare to spray or airbrush. Remember to begin by first spraying beyond the model's surface and then moving over the model in slow, steady passes to apply paint evenly. Rotate the model while painting to avoid runs and blemishes, or creating shadows around surface details.

    Set the hull aside to dry overnight. Remove the mask and repeat the process to paint the remaining area of the ship's hull.

SIMULATING WOOD

Most older vessels have wooden decks. Some historic ships may even have a wooden hull. Depending on the vessel's use or age, these features may have a bristol or worn appearance. This is yet another example of the choices available to model builders in terms of how their scale replicas can be prepared and presented.

The challenge of transforming large plastic areas into simulated wood can be accomplished in several ways. The key is to create textures and details that rival wood's natural appearance to simulate a new or worn hull and deck.

RAISED DECK LINES

Model ship decks will come molded one of two ways. They will either have raised or recessed caulking lines between each "wood" plank on the model. The idea is to accentuate this detail by darkening the caulking lines. Here's how to handle a deck with raised lines.

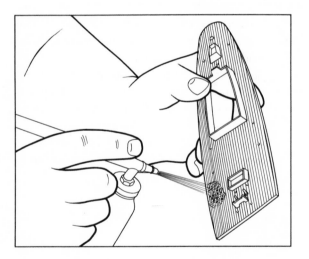

1 Prepare black lacquer paint for an airbrush. Make a solution that is a 50/50 mixture of paint and thinner. This is an occasion where the properties of lacquer are used to your advantage: This detailing method uses the etching effect of lacquer paint and thinner. Consequently, the paint will protect the deck's finish during the final step in this process.

Spray the deck with a solution of black lacquer paint and thinner. The paint will look very wet and heavy on the model. The large amount of thinner creates this look and slows down the drying process. This encourages the paint to etch into the top layer of the deck's plastic surface. After painting, set the deck aside to dry thoroughly. Be patient throughout this process.

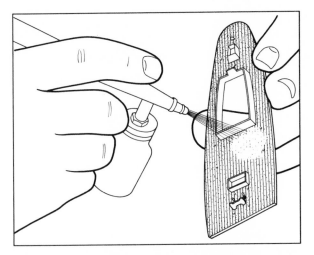 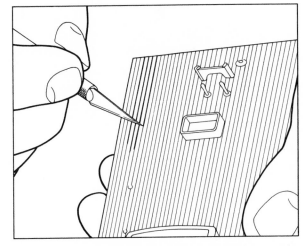

2 Clean your airbrush and select an appropriate shade of tan or light brown paint. Then prepare a paint and thinner solution that contains only 30 percent thinner.

Spray the dry black deck with the tan or light brown paint solution. Apply an even coat that creates the effect of a new deck. For a worn appearance, apply sporadic and lighter coats to the deck's surface. Set the deck aside to dry for a minimum of twenty-four hours. If possible, let it dry even longer—it is essential that the paint be completely dry for the next step.

3 Use a hobby knife with a fresh number-11 blade. Scrape the blade very lightly across the top of the raised caulking lines, using constant pressure along the surface to produce even black lines. It is better to make several passes with the knife than risk deep scrapes in the plastic. (Because the black lacquer etches into the plastic, only excessive pressure will reveal the model's original plastic.)

If you're attempting to simulate a new deck, apply a light coat of clear semigloss paint. Ignore this step if the objective is to create a worn appearance.

RECESSED DECK LINES

To paint a deck, it also is possible to create dark caulking lines with recessed details. For this tech- nique lacquer paint is not appropriate.

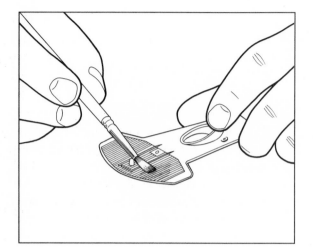

Spray paint the deck an appropriate shade of tan or brown, using a spray can or airbrush. Both will work, because it is not necessary to mix the paint before application. After painting, set the deck aside to dry completely.

Depending on the type of paint, prepare a black enamel or acrylic wash solution. Use the guidelines described on page 114 for instructions on preparing the solution.

Use a medium-size brush and apply the wash solution to the deck's surface. Make sure the solution gets into all the recessed caulking lines. For a new deck, immediately remove any excess wash solution from the surface above the caulking lines. Set the deck aside to dry. For a worn appearance, let some solution dry on the deck's surface. For an even older look, put a lighter base coat of paint on the deck first. Then spray on the correct deck color and create some wear with sporadic applications of paint.

USING A WASH FOR WOOD DETAILING

Here's another method that is especially effective for creating realistic details on the hulls of historic wooden vessels like those sailed by Christopher Columbus and other famous explorers.

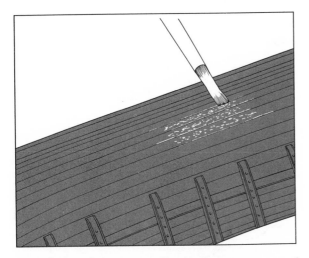

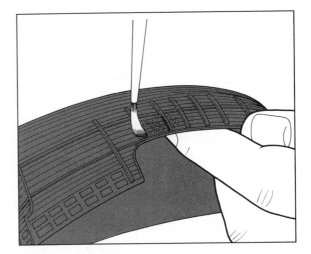

1 Select an appropriate color for the primary coat of paint. Remember to choose a color and shade that resembles wood. A little research can even reveal what kind of wood was used for the particular vessel you're building. For most ships, a good overall choice is a medium brown paint.

Spray the hull using an airbrush or spray can until it is totally covered. Set it aside to dry for twenty-four hours. A longer-than-usual drying time is necessary because this technique requires frequent handling of the model part, and therefore needs a hard, dry paint job for protection.

Now the hull is ready for a drybrush application. Refer to pages 69–70 for more details on drybrushing. Choose a lighter shade of paint in the same color family as the base coat. Medium tans are good choices for brown base colors.

Dry brush the lighter shade on the ship's hull. Be liberal (but not overly so) with this application to assure full surface coverage.

Model companies attempt to create some woodlike details during the molding process. Drybrushing highlights these details and improves their appearance. After drybrushing, other features on the ship's surface can be enhanced.

2 Prepare an india ink and isopropyl alcohol solution using the guidelines on page 68. The key to success is to ensure that the solution is not too dark, otherwise it will obscure, rather than enhance, the hull's surface details.

Test the solution on the hull before total application. If the effect is satisfactory, then apply the solution on the remaining surface of the ship's hull. Set the hull aside to dry thoroughly.

Although it first appears shiny, the india ink solution dries to a rich, semigloss patina. The final result is a plastic hull that now has the look of richly oiled wood.

MAKING SAILS

There are more possibilities for improving the appearance of old and historic sailing vessels. One dramatic effect is to replace a model kit's original plastic sails with realistic-looking fabrics. This may take a little extra time and effort, but the final model will look fabulous. Here's an effective method for replicating cloth sails.

The object in this example is to do what Christopher Columbus did at the Canary Islands with his ship *Niña*. It is on those islands that he converted the original lateen sails on his vessel to square ones for his journey to the New World in 1492.

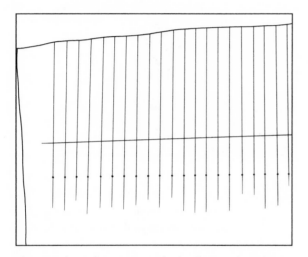

1 First, buy about one yard of polyester sheet lining from a local fabric store. Research will help determine the precise measurements of Columbus's new sails. Calculate for scale and divide that measurement by the model's scale, then transfer those dimensions to the polyester fabric you purchased. *Note*: When changing the model's sail to cloth, use the kit's original plastic sail as a template to draw on the fabric.

Trim the fabric according to the measurements you made. Leave some extra material to trim away later. Use a pencil and draw lines on the cloth sail to simulate the appearance of seams that would occur between bolts of cloth. Large sails are made from several pieces of cloth because of their large final dimensions.

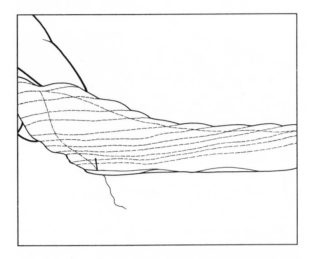

2 Sew along the seam lines with a fine tan thread. This simulates the coarse rope that joins each piece of cloth on the original sail. A sewing machine is best suited for this. If you don't have one, a local sewing center can do the work for you.

STIFFENING SAILS

The cloth is now too pliable for use as a sail on the model. It is therefore necessary to treat the cloth with a liquid that stiffens the cloth and protects it from unraveling.

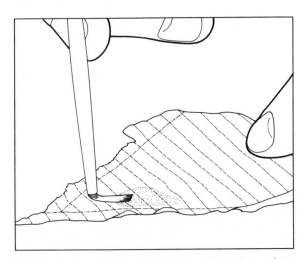

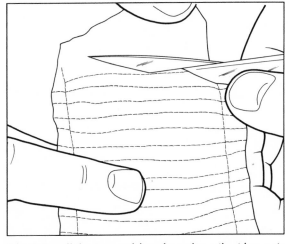

1 Prepare a solution of 20 percent white glue and 80 percent water. Add a few drops of Photo-Flo to the mixture to reduce the solution's surface tension. Photo-Flo is available at photo supply stores.

    The choice for this wetting agent is normally liquid dishwashing detergent. But Photo-Flo is best for this application because, unlike the detergent, it doesn't cause bubbles. As bubbles dry they cause rings to appear, which detracts from the sail's realistic appearance.

    Apply the solution liberally to the cloth sail with a suitable paintbrush. Don't worry about using too much. The fabric can't absorb much of the solution and there is no chance of harming the polyester material.

    Set the wet cloth sail aside to dry overnight. Once dry, the fabric sail should be as stiff as cardboard. This characteristic makes the sail easier to cut and then position on the model.

2 Trim off the excess fabric from the sail with a pair of scissors. You can create the effect of new sails by using the fabric as is.

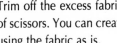

AGING SAILS

To make a model look older and more "historic," it is possible to weather the sails. Here's how to simulate a more worn appearance.

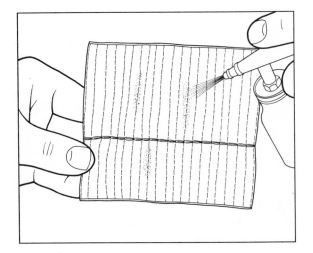

Select a neutral brown paint and make a preparation using 90 percent thinner and 10 percent paint. Prepare an airbrush for use.

Apply the paint to the sail in a streaking pattern. Do not cover the entire surface of the sail. The idea is to create stains, watermarks, and soil streaks that simulate an "out at sea" appearance.

When this application dries, attach the sail to the ship, following the model kit's instructions or the research materials you based your detailing on.

MODIFYING MASTS

Making a modification with a model kit frequently leads to other changes. This couldn't be more true than with the model of Christopher Columbus's *Niña*. To reproduce all the changes made on the Canary Islands means also that more modifications to the vessel's masts need to be made. This is necessary in order for the ship to accept its new square sails. Here's how to take those modifications one step further.

Use some research information to identify the location(s) of the new mast(s). For the *Niña*, the task at hand is to make a new mizzen mast and move the original to the foredeck position. Purchase a wooden dowel from a local hobby shop or hardware store. Match the dowel's diameter, not its length, to the kit's original mast.

Since the *Niña* now has square sails, the original mast's length is incorrect. Measure or use reference materials to calculate the mast's correct length. Approximate this measurement if you want to.

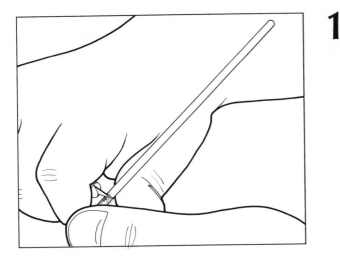

1 Cut the dowel to the appropriate length with a razor saw or similar cutting tool. Then take a hobby knife and reduce the dowel's diameter using the adzing technique described on page 74. This tapers the dowel at each end and produces a more genuine-looking mast.

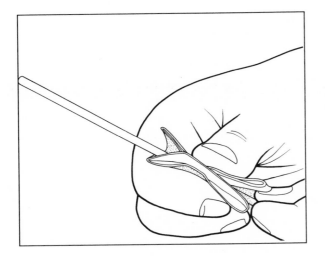

2 Use coarse sandpaper on the dowel to add texture and grain. Because this material is wood and not plastic, there is no need to wet-sand.

Follow the preceding steps for weathering the ship's wooden hull to complete the mast (page 133). Set the mast aside.

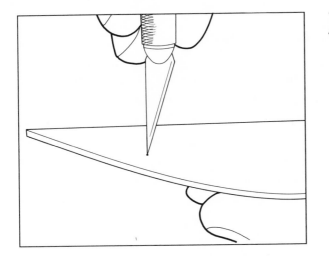

3 Calculate or approximate the location of the new mast on the ship's deck. Make a dot at this point with a pencil. Use the tip of the hobby knife's blade to create a pilot hole for the mast.

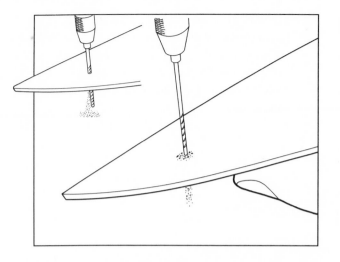

4 Change to a pin-vise tool and use the largest bit possible to drill a larger hole using the pilot hole as a guide. Put the new mast into the hole to test its fit. If it is still too small, proceed to step five.

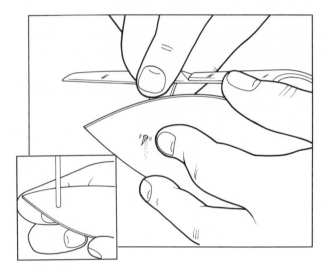

5 The idea here is to progressively increase the hole's diameter. Working too quickly can result in removing too much plastic and creating some serious filling problems later. Open a pair of scissors. Insert one blade tip into the hole and carefully ream the hole with the blade. Keep test fitting until the hole is big enough to accept the new mast. When the fit is right, attach the mast to the deck with some liquid glue.

RIGGING AND GUY WIRES

Most ships use rigging and guy wires to work the sails and to add stability to tall deck components, such as smokestacks. For many hobbyists replicating rigging and guy wires is the most challenging aspect of model ship building.

Model kits will include black thread to duplicate rigging and guy wire details. Depending on the model's scale, this thread can be the perfect size, or too "heavy-looking" to correctly replicate the real thing. Here's how to first use the original thread effectively and then substitute a material closer to scale. It takes more than two hands to attach rigging and tie knots on a model ship. Purchase some "alligator clips" from a local electronics store. These clips effectively become extra hands that help you along with this process, making the whole job less frustrating and more likely to succeed.

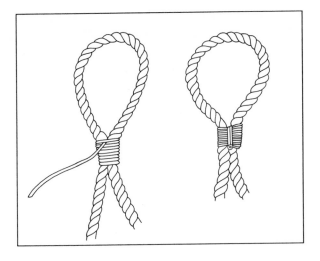

1 The instructions that come with most model kits recommend tying ordinary knots for the rigging. Although this works, it does not replicate how sailors really secure rigging to sails and tie-downs. Visit a library and get a book that shows how to tie nautical knots. Then choose a knot that is suitable, and one that you are able to tie, for the model ship. In this example, a "serving" knot is used.

Following the instructions, prepare a piece of rigging line for the ship. In case of error, always make sure to have extra line for each rigging application.

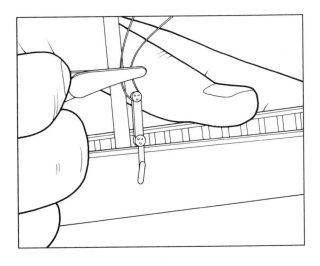

2 String the rigging through the first deadeye, or tie-down, leaving enough line for tying the knot. Use an alligator clip to secure the line to the deadeye.

Continue to set the rigging following the instructions or reference materials. Place it through the opposite deadeye and leave enough slack for another knot. Attach an alligator clip to the end of the thread to create enough line tension to hold it in place.

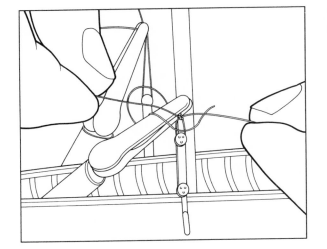

3 Return to the original deadeye and tie an appropriate knot, and repeat this step for the opposite deadeye. Don't worry about perfection—they will still look more authentic than knots with no nautical purpose. Confirm that the knots are secure and remove the alligator clips.

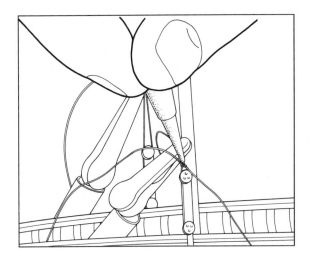

4 Apply a drop of clear modeling dope to each knot. Clear dope is available at hobby shops specializing in model planes. This will prevent the knots from working loose. After the dope dries, carefully trim off any excess thread from each knot.

GUY WIRES

Nylon thread is the perfect choice for a ship's guy wires, or if the model kit's thread is not to scale. It is available at fabric centers and comes in different diameters and a variety of colors, including clear. Here's how to use this material as guy wire for a model ship. In this example, the guy wire is an addition that improves the model's visual accuracy. A kit's box art often provides a good point of reference for the correct locations of each wire.

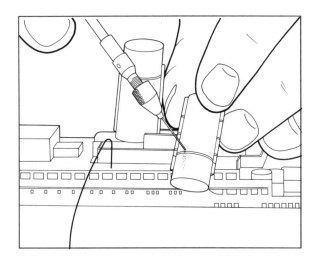

1 Estimate the scale diameter and appearance of the guy wire you want to reproduce, and purchase some transparent nylon thread from a local fabric store. On the *Titanic,* it is necessary to drill receiving holes for the guy wires. Use a pin-vise with a very fine drill bit. The idea is to create a hole just large enough to slip the nylon thread into.

Continue to drill a series of holes on the deck and stacks of the *Titanic* using the box art or photographic reference as a visual guide.

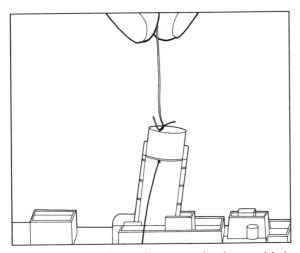

2 Get a piece of wire about six inches long and fashion a fishlike hook at one end to make a tool to retrieve the nylon thread. Keep the tool nearby for the remaining steps. Estimate the length of the guy wires and cut the correct number at least one third longer than necessary.

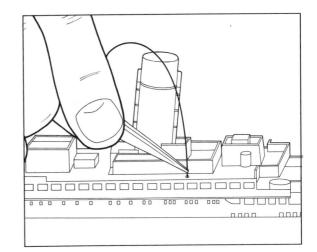

3 Put a small amount of cyanoacrylate glue into one of two receiving holes for the guy wire. In this example, the best place to start is on the deck. Insert about 1/8-inch of the nylon thread into the hole and wait for the glue to dry.

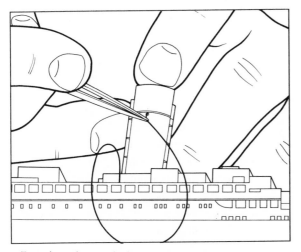

4 When dry, push the remaining thread into the appropriate hole on the stack. With a little persuasion, the thread should come up through the top of the stack. If it doesn't, use the fish hook tool you made to retrieve the nylon thread. Gently pull, and then hold, the thread taut.

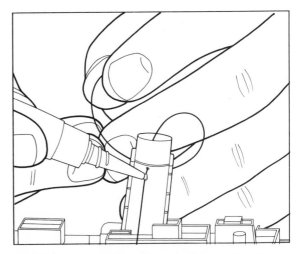

5 If you can, apply a drop of cyanoacrylate glue at this location from inside instead of outside the model part. If not, apply a small drop to the line and pull it taut. Hold the thread in place until the bond is secure. Trim off any excess, and repeat these steps for the remaining guy wires or rigging.

LIFEBOATS

Another eye-catching exterior feature on both ships and pleasure craft are lifeboats. Frequently, these model-kit parts have a molded scallop effect on the side that simulates the presence of a foul-weather cover. Sometimes the cover for the lifeboats is left off. Without a cover the scallop effect is inaccurate and becomes a visual distraction.

The first way of correcting this problem is to remove the scallops with sandpaper or a file, producing open lifeboats. A better option is to take advantage of the scallop effect and make covers for the lifeboats. Here's how to make covers for open lifeboats.

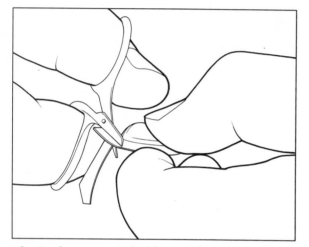

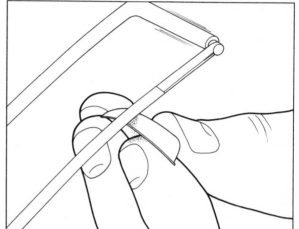

1 Purchase some 10/100ths or 10/1000ths sheet styrene from a local hobby retailer. Both thicknesses will work well but the 10/100ths sheet will yield better details.

Turn the lifeboats upside down on the sheet styrene. Leave at least a half inch or more between each boat.

Using liquid cement, glue the lifeboats to the plastic sheet. Capillary action will carry the glue along the edge of each lifeboat (page 26). Set this assembly aside to dry.

Take a pair of scissors and cut each boat away from the styrene sheet. Cut as close to the boat's edge as possible. If you are careful, it is better to substitute a hobby knife for the scissors. Remember, however, that the edge of this tool's blade increases the risk of accidentally cutting the edges of the lifeboats.

2 Use a Flex-i-file tool, file, or sandpaper to clean the edges around each lifeboat. Work slowly to avoid damaging the boats' exterior surfaces.

Now apply an appropriate painting and finishing technique of your choice to complete the lifeboats. Attach them to the main vessel following the model kit's instructions.

PAINTING DETAILS

Model ships have many small deck details. These parts come both as part of the deck and as separate pieces. In either case, use the following methods for painting small model parts.

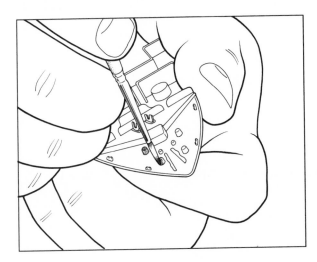

Prepare and assemble any loose deck parts following the instructions. After the assembly dries, get the deck ready for painting.

Choose an appropriate color for the ship's deck; it is a medium tan for the *Titanic.*

Use an airbrush or spray can to paint the deck. Set it aside to dry completely.

After the deck is dry, paint the other details. Use a number 0 paintbrush for this job. The tendency is to choose a finer detail brush for these small parts, but because finer brushes have too few bristles, they cannot hold and dispense enough paint for proper coverage. The number 0 brush is therefore the perfect painting tool for the job.

Use research or photographic references to select a correct color for the deck's details. Carefully paint each detail with the number 0 brush.

Examine the deck closely for any areas that need touch-ups after the deck details dry.

SKYLIGHTS

Use this painting technique for skylights.

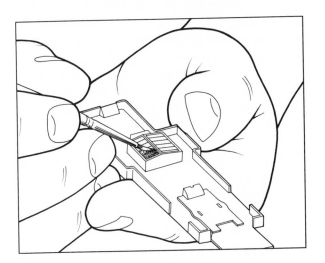

1 Paint the entire skylight white; or, skip this step if the part's original color is white.

Get a translucent blue acrylic paint, then paint the skylight and set it aside to dry thoroughly.

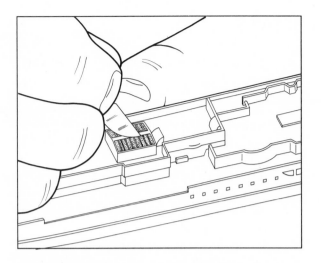

2 After it dries, take a hobby knife and gently scrape any excess blue paint from around the frame of each skylight panel. Do not use too much pressure; the object here is to remove the blue gradually without damaging the plastic until only white shows through.

The translucent blue over the white base will produce an illusion of glass in each skylight panel.

MAKING A BASE

Model ships typically come with some sort of base or stand for display. These are fine, but not nearly effective enough for displaying a vessel in its natural marine environment. Model water is easy to create and adds drama to any model ship.

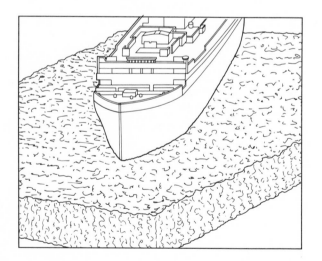

1 A piece of insulating Styrofoam about 1 inch thick, 8 inches wide, and 18 inches long is a good average size to begin building a base for most model ships. Insulating Styrofoam is available at most home building centers. Make sure the hull is right side up, and press the ship's hull down on the Styrofoam to make an indentation.

Use a sharp hobby knife and cut the foam following the outside edge of the hull's indentation. Ensure that the depth of the cut is not too high or too low in relation to the ship's waterline.

Purchase a bag of Celluclay from a local craft or hobby store. Follow the directions and prepare the Celluclay for application. When the Celluclay reaches an oatmeal-like consistency, it is ready to use.

Spread approximately a quarter-inch-thick layer of Celluclay on top of the Styrofoam base with a plastic or wooden spoon.

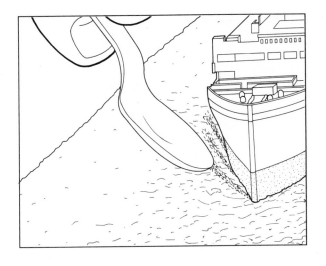

2 Put some masking or cellophane tape around the ship's hull. Make sure it's high enough to mask the model's surface from the Celluclay.

Place the ship's hull in the wet Celluclay base. Then take the plastic spoon and sculpt the Celluclay to simulate bow waves along the ship's hull. An overhead photograph of a ship underway is the best visual aid for accomplishing this effect.

3 Use a paintbrush handle on the stern of the ship to create propeller turbulence.

At a distance from the ship's hull, use the spoon to make small whitecaps and gentle waves.

Remove the hull and set the base aside to dry for two to three days. The water content of the Celluclay will affect drying time.

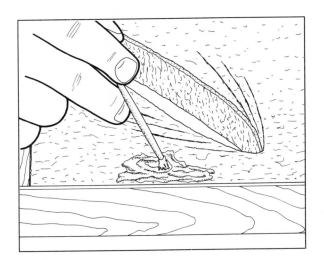

4 After the base is thoroughly dry, apply a thick layer of white glue along the entire surface of the base. The glue should fill any irregularities in the Celluclay and produce a smooth waterlike appearance.

Set this aside to dry for at least twenty-four hours.

Choose a paint color that approximates the look of water. In the example here, a bluish-gray ocean color was selected to simulate the Atlantic ocean.

Paint the Celluclay base and set it aside to dry for eight or more hours.

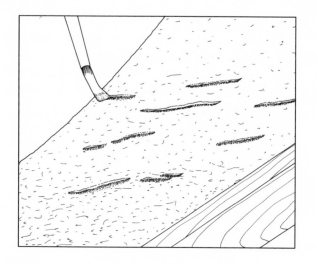

5 Highlight the crests of waves and other high-water features. Use white paint and follow the drybrushing technique described on pages 69–70. Using very light strokes, apply the paint in a manner that simulates water flowing back and away from the hull so the ship appears to be traveling forward. If the final effect is too heavy, just repaint the base its water color.

ICEBERGS

Historically, the *Titanic* struck an iceberg and eventually sank. Icebergs can be made and added as a feature to the base. Make icebergs with plaster, papier-mâché, or Styrofoam blocks. Plaster and papier-mâché icebergs are built up gradually in creating their irregular shapes. With Styrofoam blocks it is necessary to shave off material bit by bit and sculpt the iceberg into shape.

Paint model icebergs with white and silver paints to simulate the glasslike finish of arctic ice. After drying, place icebergs on the base—or slightly in it—and sculpt the "water" around their edges.

Despite their smaller selection compared with the range of other models, ships can be an exciting subject area for any model-building en-thusiast. Working on them is a great way to enhance skills and develop new ones that can be applied to any type of model.

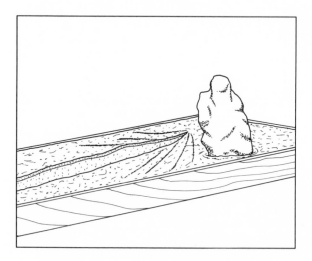

CHAPTER 19

SHOWCASING YOUR MODELS

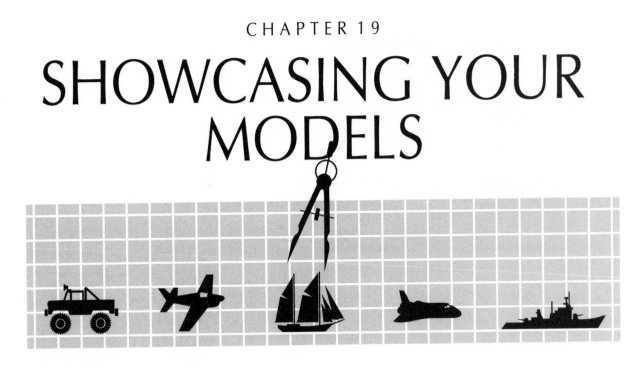

The model-building hobby goes beyond the creation of beautiful scale replicas. After completing several model kits, hobbyists need to consider the care and protection of their kits, and also consider creative options for displaying models at home.

For most model builders, displaying models on shelves is sufficient. But without a protective covering, models attract dust and can suffer harm in other ways. Use caution when choosing a display location and cleaning a model's exterior surface.

CLEANING MODELS

The most effective way to clean a model is with a soft, wide brush that has a half-inch width. Start at the highest point of the model and use gentle strokes to sweep dust off a model's surface. Be extra careful around small detail parts. Since some bonding materials—particularly white glue—weaken with age, it doesn't take much to knock off small parts.

Besides a large brush, there are two power tools available that safely do the job. One choice is a battery-operated hand-held vacuum available at hobby stores, computer stores, and some specialty shops.

The vacuum contains a small battery pack and soft bristle nozzle, and may have a vacuum bag. The tool loosens dust and sucks it into a

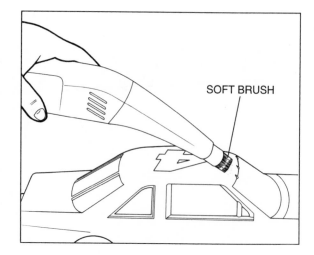

vacuum bag without dispersing the dust back into the air, the same way as its full-size cousin. Remember to work carefully around small detail parts.

The second cleaning option is to use a small household vacuum cleaner attachment. This item is available at hardware stores and houseware departments in most major retailers. This vacuum cleaner accessory has a small, soft bristle brush that is suitable for cleaning objects such as scale models.

Since it doesn't require batteries for operation, the vacuum attachment is a more economical choice. It does have more suction power and this increases the risk of accidentally removing small detail parts. Use an empty bag so that if a small part does come off, it can be retrieved from the vacuum.

PROTECTING A MODEL FROM HEAT AND SUNLIGHT

Model kits need more than periodic cleaning for their care and protection. As with photographs or similar objects, heat and sunlight can have a bad effect on a model's appearance. Common sense is the best approach in reducing a model's exposure to such elements.

No matter how cool a room may be, direct sunlight can produce enough surface heat to warp a model's surface. Continuous exposure will also fade decals and a model's exterior finish. Store models in a shaded area. Remember that the position of the earth in relation to the sun changes throughout the year and that a shaded location may not always be that way.

When looking for a storage location, be aware of heating and cooling vents. Besides throwing airborne particles on a model's surface, heat also can harm exterior finishes and decals. Just remember how much time and effort originally went into building a model, and invest a little more time into finding the right location for display.

DISPLAY CASES

Besides efforts to protect and care for your models, there is nothing more threatening than a pair of curious hands. The only protection against this kind of potential harm is storage in a display case. It is also a good shield against dust and heat from heating and cooling vents.

There are several types of commercially available model display cases. Although some manufacturers may recommend cases for their own car-model kits, they can be used for others, too. For example, one manufacturer makes three case sizes for its brand of model cars. With some imagination, and a few measurements, a model builder can easily determine which can also be used for another brand or subject.

There are many other places besides your local hobby shop to look for display cases. Visit local model railroad shops, model train shows,

jewelry supply stores, or contact commercial display companies. Any one of these may have the perfect case at an affordable price for displaying a favorite model kit.

MAKING A DISPLAY CASE

If a suitable display case isn't available commercially, then it is also possible to make an attractive homemade display case. Here are some general ideas for making a basic case.

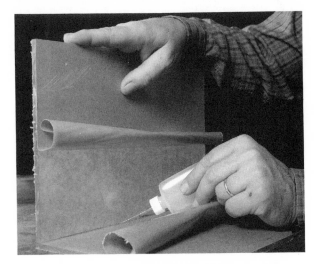

Calculate the length, width, and height of the display case. Make sure to leave some extra room with all the dimensions to create safe clearance around the model. Go to a local building center, glass supplier, or hardware store and select an appropriate thickness of Plexiglas.

A Plexiglas ranging from 3/16 inch to 1/8 inch thickness is generally ideal for a display case. Ask the retailer to cut the sheet to the precise measurements. Even if there is an extra charge for this service it assures a safe and accurate cut.

Assemble the case using an acrylic bonding agent or Super Glue. Set it aside to dry to allow the glue to form a secure bond between its pieces.

MAKING A BASE

To make a base, use plywood, particle board, or shelving material. The key is to make a secure base that supports the acrylic cover. The choice of wood for the base depends on personal preference, cost, and availability.

Here are two methods for making a base that will securely support a case.

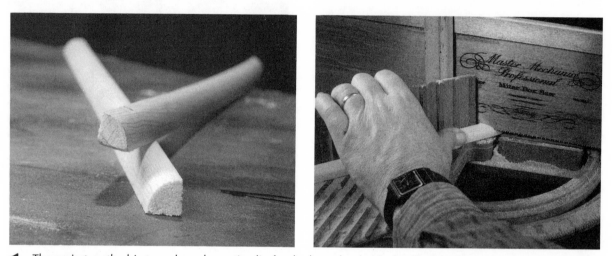

1 The easiest method is to make a decorative lip for the base that holds the Plexiglas top in place. Go to a local building center or lumberyard and purchase some quarter-round trim. Another option is to buy balsa wood quarter round from a local hobby store.

    Using the top's outside dimensions plus the width of the quarter-round trim, cut the base to size.

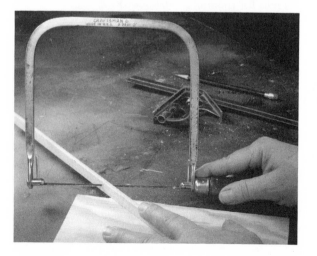

2 Cut the quarter-round to size and attach it to the base using white glue and finishing nails.

3 Finish the base by painting or staining it. A pleasing effect can be achieved by staining or painting the trim a color that contrasts or complements the primary color of the base. Set the base aside to dry overnight.

ANOTHER METHOD FOR MAKING A BASE

A second choice for securing the top in place is to rout a groove into the top of the base. There are two ways to do this.

Get a router and make a groove in the base. Cut a groove on the base that equals the outside dimensions of the top but slightly larger than the thickness of the Plexiglas. Use your judgment to decide the depth of the groove.

You can also take the base to a lumberyard, or carpenter, and pay a nominal fee to have the groove made for you. If you don't have a router, this is your only choice.

Finish the base with paint or stain that complements the presentation and colors of your model.

A display case is a good way to protect a model, but remember that there is little ventilation inside the case and heat can be trapped. Keep the case away from direct sunlight and other heat-causing sources.

MAKING A DIORAMA

Another way to show off a model is by making a diorama. A diorama is a scene that places models in their natural environment. It can be a flat base, with or without a Plexiglas cover, that duplicates realistic surface details. A diorama also can sim-ulate a three-dimensional perspective by incorporating painted sides and a back wall.

Here's how to produce realistic presentation environments for a variety of scale models.

FABRICATING DIORAMA BASES

1 A simple but realistic base design produces a street scene for model cars. All that is required is some paint and a little imagination.

Prepare a base following the steps on pages 150–151. Seal the surface of the base with paint or another appropriate finish that produces some texture.

After the sealing material dries, apply a coat of black paint to simulate an asphalt road. Flat black is preferable, but semigloss and gloss will also work. Set the base aside to dry thoroughly.

To create a sidewalk, calculate the thickness and width in relation to the road and the scale of the model.

2 Cut a strip of wood to the correct dimensions (balsa wood often works well for this effect). Paint the wood strip gray or tan, or sand it to duplicate the natural color of a sidewalk. Set the strip aside to dry, if necessary.

3 For extra detail, add yellow center lines to the road's surface. The first option is to paint the line detail using normal or reverse-masking techniques (pages 93–94). Reverse masking is the best choice when the primary paint is a dark color.

Another way to create center lines is with thin Chart-Pak tape. This tape comes in a variety of colors that include yellow and white. The width correctly simulates roadway lines for most scales as well as some of today's new roadway-surface marking systems. Cut the tape's length to size, and trim the width if necessary, using a hobby knife. Apply it to the base.

Use some white glue to attach the wooden sidewalk(s) to the base in preparation for the model.

These detailing techniques offer the simplest approach to making a realistic base for the presentation of a model car. More involved detailing can simulate "pit row" at a racetrack or traffic signals, and can include scale model figures as pedestrians or spectators. Only your skills and imagination will •limit the complexity of your projects.

CREATING A NATURAL ENVIRONMENT

For kits with military vehicles, off-road vehicles, and animal figures, creating a natural environment is the best choice for a diorama base. Here's how to simulate natural occurring features for a variety of subjects.

Prepare a base suitable for the model's scale using the guidelines on pages 150–151. Purchase some scenic materials from a model railroad shop. There is a wide selection of scenic supplies to choose from including trees, rocks, and lichen. Use photographic references as guides to choose the correct textures, colors, and plant growth to replicate the environment you're building.

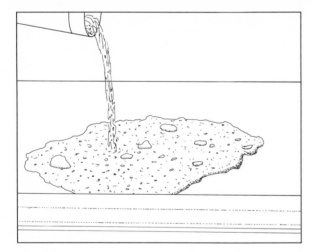

1 Get some Celluclay and mix it accordingly, remembering that an oatmeal consistency works the best. Apply approximately a quarter-inch-thick coat of Celluclay to the base using a plastic spoon to create surface contours that simulate an irregular, natural terrain. Set the base aside to dry for twenty-four to forty-eight hours.

Select the primary ground color and paint the base. Tans to medium browns will always produce good earth tones. After applying the paint, set the base aside to dry thoroughly.

Make a white glue preparation of 80 percent glue and 20 percent water, along with a few drops of liquid dishwashing detergent as a wetting agent. Apply this solution to the base of the model.

Take some scenic "ground" material and apply it over the white glue. Use your discretion in creating heavier layers, letting the primary color enhance the appearance. Set this assembly aside to dry.

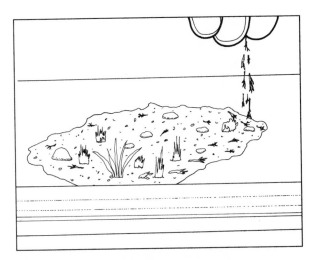 

2 Add some greenery for shrubs, vegetation, or trees. Your selection depends on photographic references and personal discretion. Adhere all materials to the base with the white glue solution.

3 The display in this example is designed for a triceratops dinosaur. To improve realism, footprints and dinosaur egg details have been added.

Make footprints immediately after the first ground cover application. Before the material dries, use the model dinosaur's foot to gently make depressions in appropriate locations. Rinse any ground cover off the model's surface.

Eggs are a cinch to duplicate. Find a suitable material closely resembling the shape and size of an egg. Dry navy beans are the best choice for triceratops. Placing them in a nest further adds to the realism of the setting.

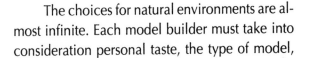

The choices for natural environments are almost infinite. Each model builder must take into consideration personal taste, the type of model, building skills, and research materials in deciding what materials to use. Don't be afraid to experiment with inexpensive scenic materials.

CREATING BACKGROUNDS

A diorama can have greater three-dimensional impact with the presence of a suitable background. Making a backdrop for a display can range in difficulty. An expert artist can hand paint detailed backgrounds with an airbrush. But for most model builders, the simplest method is probably the best choice. Here's an easy way to make a background for most model-kit subjects.

1 A popular choice for a background is a sky. Go to a local art supply store and purchase some sky blue or white poster board. Paint a white board sky blue.

Add some clouds to improve the board's visual impact. Use a spray can, or preferably an airbrush, to add cloud details to the poster board. You don't have to be an artist to paint clouds. Set it aside to dry.

2 Cut the board to the appropriate size for the model's diorama base (pages 150–151). Use white glue to attach the poster board around the base's sides and back. Run a bead of glue along each corner to secure the edges. The diorama is ready after the glue sets up.

APPLYING SCENIC BACKDROPS

For more visual detail, scenic backdrops are available to replicate a variety of environments. The choices can include a city skyline, a water-front, an industrial area, or several rural scenes. For success, be patient when applying these backgrounds.

1 Visit a local hobby retailer and purchase a background scene suitable for the model and its diorama.

After visiting the hobby shop, stop by an art supply store and buy some "artist's board" or Bristol board, not poster board. Bristol board is a firmer material that works best for this application. Also purchase a can of spray adhesive.

Cut the board into three pieces equaling the width of the diorama's back and sides respectively. Cut the board's height equal to the backdrop's height. If this is too high, trim the backdrop accordingly taking care not to damage its appearance. Measure and cut the scene to cover each individual piece of board. Mark each piece for positioning—such as right, left, and center.

2 Lay the board flat on a worktable. Spray the adhesive sparingly on to the board's surface, following the instructions on the can.

Note: Using the adhesive only on the board will make it easy to remove the backdrop after it dries. Applying the adhesive to both the board *and* the background creates a permanent bond that prevents removal without damage.

3 Place the backdrop scenes on the board and carefully align the edges where details meet. This is especially important for buildings and other eye-catching features. To avoid imperfections, roll the scenic material back and start at one edge. Slowly unroll the scene onto the board while pushing out any air bubbles that appear.

Apply the three scenery boards to the diorama with an appropriate bonding agent. Carpenter's wood glue is a good choice for this procedure. Lay a small bead of white glue along the corners to seal the edges of the board.

Dioramas can be as fun and challenging as building models. With the broad range of materials, the only limitations are the skill and imagination of the model builder. Accept the challenge and find ways to create presentations just like the ones in the finest museums.

The joy of this hobby is its variety of subjects and the opportunity to make a model unique. Remember that skill, technique, and patience are the most essential ingredients for success with any project. Think of each little setback as only part of the learning process. And don't be afraid to experiment and take some risks.

The techniques shown in this book are not exclusive to any particular model. Think about how they can apply to the model you want to build more than anything. Enjoy the adventure and the fun that this hobby has to offer.

ACKNOWLEDGMENTS

It's important that we recognize the people whose individual contributions made this book possible. Tom Clark, executive producer for the television show, had tremendous faith in our ability to sucessfully write this book. Jim Conway, Mike's employer, was once again generous to allow him to dedicate time within work's daily demands.

The team of Teri DeBruhl, photographer, Charlie Inglett, art director, and Dan Greshel created beautiful color photographs. They also provided prints for many of this book's vital illustrations. In addition, Don Fouché selected over 200 video still frames that effectively demonstrate many techniques.

The contributions of our master model builders are spread throughout the book. We sincerely thank them for years of creative work and exceptional model building: Bill Devins, Jerry Taylor, Ed Chesley, Alan Jones, Jim Kelly, Mike Fleckenstein, Brenda Hemsley, Mike and Ron Dobrzelecki, Jack Kennedy, Doris Reeves, Bob Schleicher, Ron Cole, Dave Chamberlain, Sue Lefferts, and Trip Anderson. We extend an additional thank you to Bob Watson, who organized every aspect of the model building for the television show.

There would be no book without the *Adventures in Scale Modeling* public television series. Over the years many professionals helped make the television show what it is today. To all of you at South Carolina ETV, WSWP-TV, Beckley, West Virginia, and everyone associated with the show, we hope this book reflects the dedication and skill you brought to the television series.

Finally we thank our families and friends. Their patience, understanding, and support kept us going when we needed it most. Enjoy the book, watch the show when you can, and good luck with the hobby!

INDEX

161

glue, 17–22
    applying of, 18, 25, 29
    block for, 24
    brushes for 24–25
    capillary action and, 26, 28, 142
    carpenter's, 158
    chrome details and, 31
    epoxy, 72
    evaporation and, 24
    glue tip for, 18, 29
    liquid solvent, 23–26, 28, 30–31, 142
    toothpick and palette technique for, 19, 21–22, 30
    tube, 17–19, 24, 29–30
    ventilation and, 17, 21, 23
    white, 20–21, 32, 111, 135, 145
glue pens, 27–28
guy wires, 138–141

helicopters, 88

icebergs, 146
india ink, 68, 114, 133
instruction sheets, 13, 14
    paint recommendations on, 37
instrument panels, 82–86
irregular surfaces, 128
isopropyl (rubbing) alcohol, 68, 133

kit bashing, 98–99
kits, 12–15
    choosing of, 13
    commemorative, 12
    identifying contents of, 14–15
    instruction sheets and, 13, 14, 37
    manufacturers' flaws in, 33
    rare, 13
    scale and, 13
    skill level and, 12–13
Krazy Glue, 20, 21, 61

lacquer paint:
    deck lines and, 132
    "etching" by, 42
    masking tape and, 95
    silver finishes with, 93–94
large-scale models, 76
latex, 40
leather, 60, 62
lettering:
    dry-transfer, 64–65

on tires, 63
lifeboats, 142–143
lighting, 1, 3
liquid solvents, 23–26
    applying of, 25–26, 30–31
    capillary action and, 26, 28, 142
    evaporation and, 24
    in glue pens, 28
long-nose side cutters, 9

Mary Jane's Defense Weekly, 55
masking tape, 10, 30, 87
    cellophane tape and, 100
    irregular surfaces and, 128
    lacquer paint and, 95
    large areas and, 129
    notebook paper as substitute for, 95, 129
masts, 136–138
metallic paint, 73–75, 78
metallic surfaces, 90–95
    Bare-Metal foil for, 90–91
    of cars, 73–75, 78
    painting, 92, 93–94
military vehicles, 106–122
    antennas of, 106–109
    camouflage netting for, 115–116
    engine vents of, 114
    "heavy" details on, 107
    individualizing of, 117
    painting camouflage on, 113
    small parts and, 117–118
    suspension modification and, 111–112
    weld line on, 110–111
Minwax, 58
model holders:
    from coat hangers, 74
    making of, 61
modeling dope, 140
modeling knives, 7–8
model putty, 33–34
Model Ship Builder, 125
mold-release agent, 15
motor tools, 10
    removing excess putty with, 34
music wire, 107

nail clippers, 9
Nautical Research Guild, 125
netting, camouflage, 115–116
Niña, 134, 136
notebook paper, 95, 129

For a copy of the *Adventures in Scale Modeling* product catalog, listing all of the television programs, special videos, and other merchandise, call **1–800–553–7752**, or write to:

SCETV MKT
Box 11,000
Columbia, SC 29211

No matter what your interest or skill level, you'll find something of value in the *Adventures in Scale Modeling* catalog!